k

the ju jitsu handbook

Roy Inman OBE 8TH Dan

Published by SILVERDALE BOOKS
An imprint of Bookmart Ltd
Registered number 2372865
Trading as Bookmart Ltd
Blaby Road
Wigston
Leicester LE18 4SE

D&S Books Ltd
Kerswell,
Parkham Ash, Bideford
Devon, England
EX39 5PR

e-mail us at:-
enquiries@dsbooks.fsnet
enquiries@dsbooks.fsnet.co.uk

This edition printed 2004
ISBN 1-84509-042-X

DS0126. Ju Jitsu Handbook

Creative Director: Sarah King
Editor: Nicky Barber
Project editor: Anna Southgate
Designer: Debbie Fisher
Photographer: Paul Forrester

Fonts: Helvetica, Eurostile

Printed in China

1 3 5 7 9 10 8 6 4 2

contents

introduction:

Ju Jitsu history and origins

Ju jitsu is practised throughout the world, where it is known variously as jiujitsu, jiujutsu, jujutsu and jujitsu. All names refer to the same martial art. Whatever the spelling, the meaning is the same. Ju jitsu literally means 'gentle art' (ju meaning 'gentle' and jitsu meaning 'art'). Ju jitsu is a grouping term for various traditional Japanese martial arts.

The basics of ju jitsu include elements such as pushing, pulling, kicking, tripping and hitting with the open hand – a term that means without weapons, although the hand itself may be a fist, open, or gripping. More complex techniques such as punching, locks, holds, throws and defensive manoeuvres are also used, although learning them requires perseverance.

The objective of ju jitsu is to neutralise an attack by any method as quickly as possible. Ju jitsu training deals with real-life situations, so although in practice there are rules and safety considerations, ju jitsu can be very brutal. If you are faced with a real life-and-death situation your personal safety becomes the key focus. Ju jitsu teaches you how to defend yourself and, if the need arises, to counter-attack. This book deals with various scenarios, but possible situations are limitless so practice is necessary to enable a strong base knowledge to deal with the unexpected.

Although many traditionalists dismiss ju jitsu as a sport there is a sporting aspect to modern-day ju jitsu. Those who compete do so under predetermined rules which dictate the level of contact and suitable areas that can be targeted. There are different ju jitsu organisations and the rules vary between each one.

I hope this book offers an insight into ju jitsu. However, it should be used as a learning tool, in addition to, not in exclusion of, instruction from a trained jujitsuka sensei (coach).

The history of ju jitsu

Ju jitsu is a group term for many fighting forms that have been taught and practised in Japan since time immemorial. It was developed from many different teachings that either originated in Japan, or were brought to Japan from nearby countries, each master teaching his own learned and adapted techniques.

Establishing the exact dates and origins of martial arts is a complex task because many masters would not readily reveal their knowledge. Often masters of martial arts passed on their wisdom, knowledge and techniques to only a privileged few. It was rare for traditional fighting techniques to be recorded. Instead, knowledge was passed on by word of mouth – and even then there was an element of secrecy. It was common for masters to withhold key elements of their knowledge to be shared only with an approved successor. If no suitable candidate was found, the knowledge died with the master, unless the master's followers were able to rediscover the technique or techniques.

Ancient history

It is impossible to pinpoint exactly when ju jitsu came into existence because it has many different origins. However, an ancient Japanese legend tells of two gods, Kajima and Kadori, who are said to have reprimanded the unruly inhabitants of an eastern province using ju jitsu.

In 2674BC, a Chinese monk called Huang-Di founded wu-su, meaning martial arts. His concept involved the use of the body in order to defend oneself. Open-handed techniques were also reported to have been used in 772BC in China. In 230BC chikura kurabe, a wrestling

sport, became integrated into ju jitsu training [?also in China??]. In AD525, a Buddhist monk [?name?] is said to have travelled from India to China where he combined Chinese kempo (known as kenpo in Japan) with yoga breathing. He eventually developed this technique into go-shin-jutsu-karate, meaning 'self-defence art of the open hand'.

In Japan, there is evidence of the existence of open-handed techniques during the Heian period (AD794–1185). These techniques were used in conjunction with weapons training for the samurai warriors. In AD880 the Daito-ryu Aiki Ju-Jitsu School was founded by Prince Teijun. This school taught secret shugendo techniques, and these eventually became the basis of kendo, using circular hand movements to combat against an assailant with weapons. In 1532 Hisamori Tenenuchi formed the Tenenuchi Ryu School of ju jitsu in Japan, and he has received much of the accreditation for founding the formal art of ju jitsu. Many fighting techniques taught at the Tenenuchi Ryu school in Japan originated from a more ancient form of combat, sumai (an ancient form of sumo). Many other similar systems, differing slightly in points of emphasis and in name, were formulated around that time. In 1559, a monk called Chin Gen Pinh migrated from China to Japan bringing with him the art of kempo. Certain aspects of kempo became integrated into present day ju jitsu. Ju jitsu flourished throughout the Tokugawa era in Japan as it was an integral part of samurai training.

It was not until the 1900s that Japanese masters took their combative skills abroad. Then ju jitsu was one of the first martial arts to be seen in Western society. At specially organised displays jujitsuka demonstrated their amazing power and control, encouraging challengers including those trained in boxing and wrestling – sometimes even two at a time! Westerners had never seen such effective and complex manoeuvres. Most challengers were reduced to submission or had to withdraw due to injury.

Other martial arts

After the Tokugawa era, ju jitsu began to decline. At the same time, other martial arts, many devised from ju jitsu, were increasing in popularity. These other martial arts had limited scope and structure, and this set them apart from ju jitsu.

In 1882 Jigoro Kano, an expert in ju jitsu and an educationalist formulated the sport of judo, 'the gentle way', from specifically selected aspects of ju jitsu. Jigoro Kano removed the aspects of ju jitsu that he believed to be dangerous and introduced new techniques and principles; he also succeeded in increasing the popularity of martial arts. Aikido 'the way of spirit and mind' also has its roots in ju jitsu. General Shinra Saburo Yoshimutsu, a general in the Japanese army, devised from ju jitsu a pure form of educational exercises as a way of advancing his military officers mentally, physically and spiritually.

It was known as Daitoryu Aiki Ju jitsu and was kept secret and passed down only to a hereditary successor until 1910, when Dr Morihei Ueshiba received the knowledge. He took what he felt were the best techniques of Daitoryu Aiki Ju jitsu and combined them with techniques from other forms of ju jitsu to create present-day aikido. Certain styles of karate, especially kenpo karate, have also taken techniques from ju jitsu.

Aikido is primarily based on the momentum and pressure-point aspects of ju jitsu.

Ju jitsu has been divided up into separate martial arts. The reason for this was possibly that ju jitsu became too multifaceted and there was too much to learn; or it may have been because there was no structured way of teaching ju jitsu so that it was too complicated to learn. As a result, ju jitsu is often broken down into three component arts: judo, involving the throwing and ground grappling aspects of ju jitsu; karate, with its punches and kicks; and aikido which uses the principles of momentum and pressure points.

Despite its decline, ju jitsu has survived into the present day. Some martial artists study ju jitsu per se, some learn the component parts separately, gaining proficiency in each area and piecing ju jitsu back together in their own way, and others specialise in one element, for example judo, karate or aikido.

Judo involves the throwing and ground-grappling aspects of ju jitsu.

Many styles of ju jitsu currently exist throughout the world. Ju jitsu is a tool for survival. It teaches a variety of techniques, and students are encouraged to react to whatever situation presents itself rather than simply matching specific defences to specific moves. From the base techniques, a jujitsuka is able to develop new moves, combinations and responses. With practice, these moves become second nature.

A jujitsuka never knows what kind of attacks will present themselves, so has to control fear and apprehension. This involves the mental and spiritual aspects of ju jitsu. Traditional teachings develop ki, the inner spirit, a person's drive or energy, enabling jujitsuka to take control of a situation in a relaxed manner. This takes much practice to acquire. With knowledge and skill, confidence is also built. Jujitsuka learn to use pressure points and are able to control the amount of pain inflicted. As a result, emphasis is placed on non-violence. It is unnecessary for a jujitsuka to provoke a situation which could otherwise be avoided, therefore physical confrontation is an indication that it was not possible to resolve the situation in a non-violent manner.

Modern-day ju jitsu is practised in a safe environment in which jujitsuka are taught how to control techniques so that they don't inflict damage. In competitive ju jitsu there are strict rules specifying what areas of the opponent's body can and cannot be targeted. It works on a point-scoring basis. Points are scored for blows, kicks, strikes, throws, holds, locks and strangles (dependant on the particular rules of the event). There are also varying degrees of contact ranging from touch-contact and semi-contact through to full contact.

You can never be prepared

for the unexpected no matter how alert you are; it is how you deal with the situation when it arises that is important. Ju jitsu teaches jujitsuka primarily how to avoid an attack. If this is not possible, the attack is deflected using a block, and/or a counterattack. Unlike judo, ju jitsu is not about throwing an opponent and following to the ground for a hold-down. It is about ensuring your own safety – so why follow into a hold-down when you can strike the assailant and escape in one piece!

chapter 1:

Training basics: safety and etiquette

To achieve skills in ju jitsu you need to practise throws and joint locks with a partner. For optimum safety you need to learn how to fall correctly. You also need to know what the submission signals are, and when you should give them.

Dojo and tatame

Ju jitsu is practised in a dojo. A tatame (mat) is usually used for safety when training, particularly for throwing and ground work. Of course, a real-life fighting situation could occur anywhere!

The ju jitsu tatame, or mat, has to be of sufficient density to absorb the force of the body landing on it. All walls and obstacles should be covered in protective material.

Judogi and zori

Ju jitsu is usually practised wearing a gi, consisting of trousers, jacket and a belt. The theory behind this is that, if attacked, an attacker is highly likely to be clothed. However, everyday clothes would not be able to withstand frequent training sessions.

A jujitsuka usually trains with bare feet. Traditionally, zori were worn to and from the place of practice. Zori are similar to flip-flops but made from straw.

The loose-fitting gi allows freedom of movement.

Etiquette

Respect is a major part of ju jitsu. A jujitsuka should respect his or her sensei (coach) and other jujitsuka. Rei (bow) is an expression of respect and consideration signified by a standing (ritsurei) or kneeling bow (zarei). A jujitsuka performs a ritsurei when entering and leaving the dojo, and a zarei as a group to the highest grade at the beginning and end of a practice. A jujitsuka always bows to an opponent before and after a practice. The philosophy behind this is to show respect for your place of training, your sensei, your opponents and ju jitsu itself. Other factors such as hygiene and self-discipline are fundamental aspects of ju jitsu.

Zarei

Starting position.

Full rei position.

Zarei cont'd

Start position for kneeling bow.

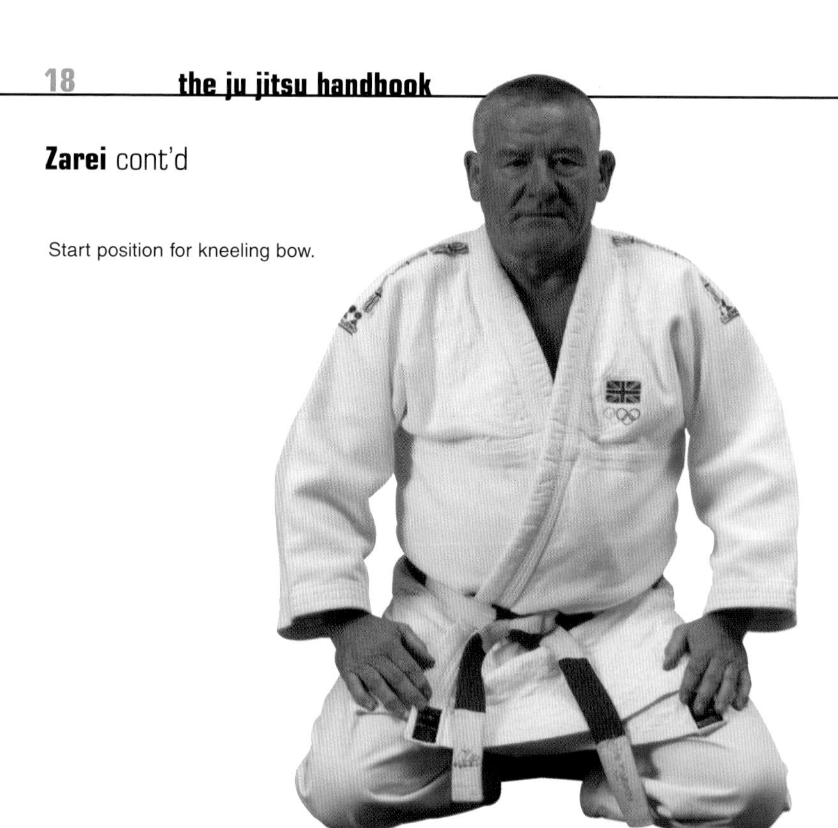

Full kneeling bow.

Ritsurei

Start position for standing bow.

Full standing bow.

Ritsurei cont'd

Front view for standing bow.

Front view of full standing bow.

Submission

When practising elbow locks, wrist locks, knee locks and strangles, a partner can submit so as not to be injured or permanently damaged. This submission is indicated by a double tap of the hand on tori's body (usually the arm, back or leg) or by double tapping the ground or mat with either the hand or foot. As a last resort a verbal submission "Matte!" can be used, meaning "I give up". However, in a real life-threatening situation there is no such thing as "I give up"!

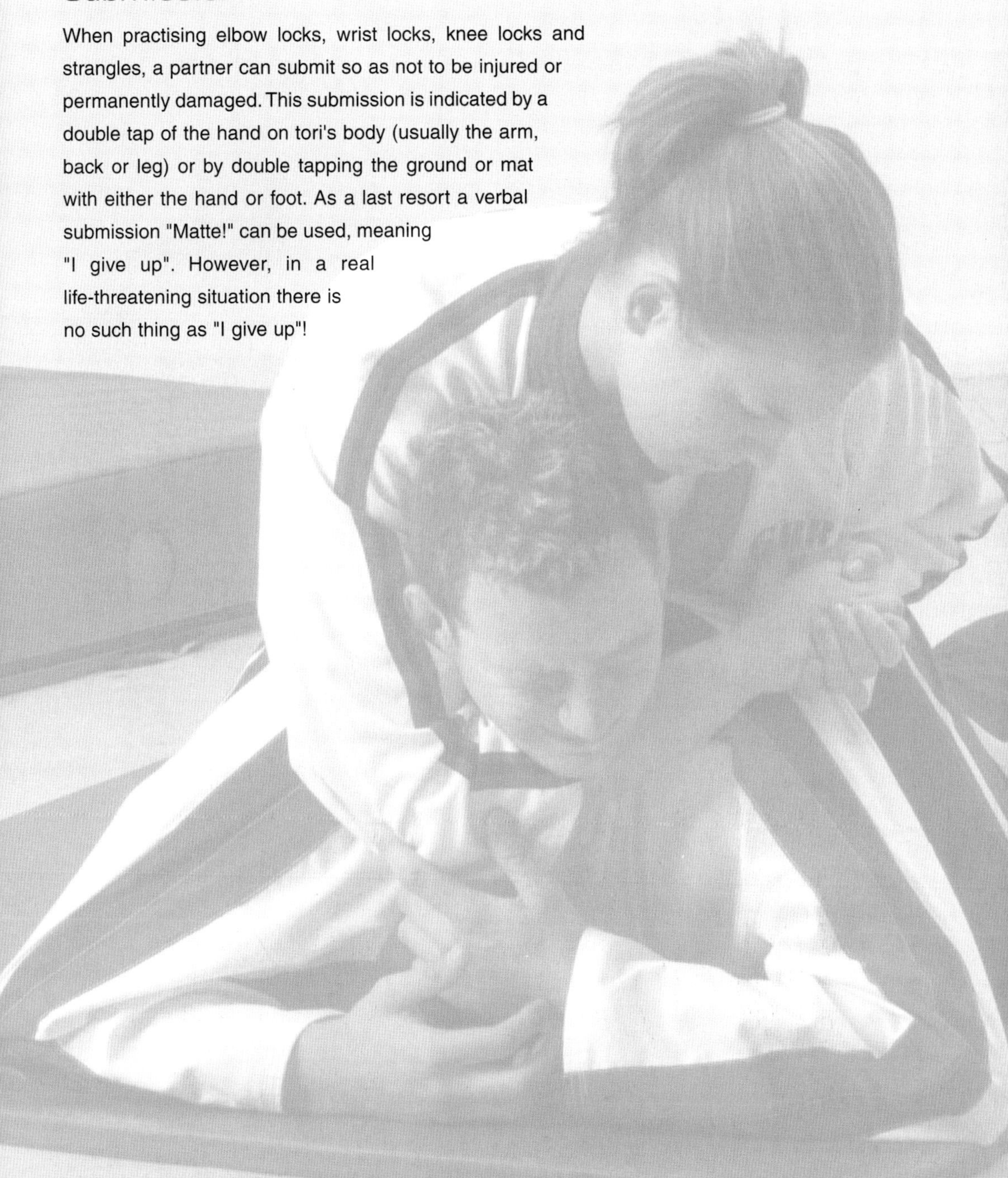

Defences to attacks

All techniques in this book are demonstrated to the right; this is done to prevent confusion. However, if you are left-handed these techniques can be converted accordingly i.e. substitute 'right' for 'left' in the explanations. In fact, it is useful to practise techniques on both sides as this helps to prevent any muscular imbalances and serves to confuse an assailant.

The person who is being attacked is called uke. However, when the person being attacked defends him or herself, he or she then becomes tori (the person executing the technique). To save confusion, in this book tori will always be used to indicate the jujitsuka who is responding to an attack. Uke will refer to the jujitsuka who is being countered, despite his or her original attack.

The major objective of the ju jitsu throw invariably requires uke to land flat on the back and, depending on the surface uke is landing on (ie concrete or hard wood), this can serioulsy wind or damage him or her. Uke is certainly in a disorientated state, even if not seriously injured, and tori should follow through with an atemi waza technique (straight punch or kick) while uke is in this position. Uke can also be thrown on to the head or shoulder joint, rendering him or her unconscious or incapacitated.

Terminology

Uke is the aggressor, on whom the counter manoeuvre is performed.

Tori is the person responding to the initial attack and executing the final technique.

Waza means technique (i.e. atemi waza: striking technique; nage waza: throwing technique; tachi waza: standing technique; newaza: ground technique).

Ukemi waza
(breakfall techniques)

Ukemi waza or breakfall techniques are specifically designed moves used to protect the body when being thrown. These breakfall techniques are one of the major training aids for the throwing elements of ju jitsu. Ukemi allow throwing techniques to be practised without the risk of injury. It takes a lot of practice to allow the body to relax as you are being thrown – the initial reaction tends to be to tense up.

Breakfall techniques are usually first practised close to the ground to lessen the impact and to allow the jujitsuka to gain confidence and the correct technique before advancing to an upright position. It is important to learn breakfalls on both sides, as an opponent could be left- or right-handed, or even ambidextrous. In order to learn these techniques correctly, beginners should seek the advice and guidance of a qualified ju jitsu sensei (or judo sensei).

Backward breakfall

Stage 1

Stage 2

Stage 1

The jujitsuka lies flat on his back, with knees bent and with his back flat against the tatame, placing his arms across his body and then slapping the mat, making sure to keep his arms straight by his side as he performs the slap.

Stage 2

The jujitsuka crouches down with arms straight by her sides (the tips of the fingers can be used to maintain balance). He then rolls backwards and as his back touches the mat he slaps the mat.

Side breakfall

This is a single-arm breakfall. From a squat position the jujitsuka pushes one leg across in front of the other and rolls on to his side. On contact with the mat the jujitsuka slaps it with his free arm. Once confidence is built this can be performed from a standing position.

A useful training drill for the side breakfall can be done in pairs. Uke is on his hands and knees, in a press-up position, tori reaches under uke's body, takes his far arm and pulls it through, maintaining her grip in order to support uke. As uke spins round he slaps the mat in a side breakfall. This drill relies on tori's support.

Start position.

The side-breakfall action.

Forward-rolling breakfall

The action is similar to a forwards roll. However, unlike in gymnastics, in ju jitsu it is important that the head does not touch the mat for safety reasons, therefore this type of roll is executed to the jujitsuka's diagonal and it is the shoulder, not the head, that makes contact with the tatame. Starting in an upright position, the jujitska places one foot forward (it is usually best to learn this on the dominant side first and progress on to the other side). The jujitsuka reaches forward using the arm on the same side of the body as the leg. The jujitsuka turns his hand under towards his body (it is advisable to take the advice of a ju jitsu sensei to ensure this is done correctly). The other hand can be used to aid balance. The jujitsuka pushes off with the back leg, the shoulder should make contact with the mat and he slaps the mat.

Flat forward breakfall

Another breakfall is when the jujitsuka falls forward with a relaxed body. The head is turned sideways so as to prevent landing on the face. The jujitsuka lands on her forearms and palms. This prevents injury and absorbs the impact of the fall. The toes are tucked under which protects the knees and torso by raising them off the mat.

Falling forward.

Landing.

chapter 2:

Atemi waza (striking techniques)

Anyone can kick or punch; these are basic instincts used for defence. However, it is important to develop the correct kicking, punching and blocking techniques in order to minimise the risk of injury. Although these techniques use the hands to punch and the legs to kick, most techniques require rotation of the hips as this is important to increase effectiveness and force. The advice of a ju jitsu sensei should be sought to learn and establish good technique.

When performing the moves in atemi waza it is essential for tori's balance to be kept stable at all times. Strikes and blows should be aimed at uke's vulnerable areas. However, it is important to remember that, when selecting an area for attack, the idea is not to aim for the surface of the opponent's body, but to punch or kick through the target area.

Tsuki waza (punching techniques)

Forming a fist

Close the hand, pulling the fingers tight into the palm. The two fingers furthest from the thumb are connected to the major muscle group in the forearm and assist with the grip and also make the wrist strong. The fist should be flexed in order to get the two striking knuckles to protrude. It is important not to leave the thumb sticking out or tuck it under the fingers, as injury may occur. The thumb wraps around the index finger pulling it in tight. The line of power should extend from the shoulder all the way through to the first two knuckles. This is achieved by ensuring that there is a straight line from the shoulder to the wrist and the top of the hand.

Choku zuki (standard fist punch)

With a clenched fist, as described above, the arm is fully extended. The impact is absorbed through the first two knuckles and the wrist stays straight in line with the forearm to prevent buckling. Following the impact, the arm is immediately pulled back. This punch is usually directed to the face or trunk.

1. Stance and hand position.

2. Punching action and finish.

3. Potential target and body position.

Screw punch

The hand is clenched in a fist with the knuckles downward. A screw action ensues: by rotating the fist 180° just prior to contact, greater force is generated. It is because of its potentially devastating effects that this type of punch is banned from boxing.

1. Stance and hand position.

2. Punching action.

3. Potential target and body position.

Haishu uchi (back-hand strike)

The move is made with a partially clenched fist with the top two joints of the thumb and fingers pulled in under the hand, keeping the rest of the hand straight.

1. Stance and hand position.

2. Punching action.

3. Potential target and position.

Uraken uchi (back-fist strike)

With a clenched fist, the back of the hand is used to slam down on the head or can be curved inwards to target the temple.

Attack to side

1. Stance and hand position.

2. Punching action.

3. Potential target and position.

Attack to head

1. Stance and hand position.

2. Punching action.

3. Potential target and position.

Tettsui uchi (hammer-fist strike)

The hand is formed into a fist and the side of the hand, along the little finger, is used to strike, usually the top of the head.

Head

1. Stance and hand position.

2. Punching action.

3. Potential target and position.

1. Stance and hand position for a side-fist punch.

2. Punching action for a straight punch.

1. Stance and hand position for a knuckle back punch.

2. Punching action for an upper-cut punch.

Teisho uchi (palm-heel strike)

Using an open hand, the heel of the hand is used to strike; the fingers can be to the side, upwards or downwards in relation to the palm heel. This technique can be used to target the face, particularly the septum of the nose, or the groin.

1. Stance and hand position.

2. Striking action.

3. Body position and strike.

Shuto uchi (Knife hand strike)

Knife hand refers to the flat open hand. The fingers and palm should be kept straight and in alignment with the wrist. This can be used to stab, using the tips of the fingers, or to chop with the edge of the hand. The hand can be held vertically or horizontally for a stabbing motion, this can be aimed at the aggressor's groin, stomach, throat or specific targets on the face. A chopping action can be delivered with the hand held with the palm upwards using the side of the hand, or with the palm downwards, using the index finger edge of the hand. This can be directed to the side of the neck, face or the floating ribs.

1. Stance and hand position.

2. Striking action.

Palm up

1. Stance and hand position.

2. Striking action.

3. Body position and strike.

Side palm down

1. Stance and hand position.

2. Striking action.

3. Body position and strike.

Hand-striking actions

1. Stance and hand position for hammer punch.

2. Striking action for knife hand strike.

Keri waza
(kicking techniques)

Kicks are usually aimed low as they are safer to execute. As a rule of thumb, the higher you kick, the less stable you become. Furthermore, a high kick can be countered by a jujitsuka, and if a leg is caught you can be thrown to the ground. It is also important that tori's balance is secure, which can be difficult, as most kicks are performed on one leg. Successful kicking techniques rely on considerable flexibility of the groin and hip, and it is important to learn correct technique when kicking or punching.

Mae geri (front kick)

The knee is raised to waist level and the foot extended forward, making contact with the target area; this can be executed using the toes, the ball of the foot or the heel. The lower leg is brought back to the vertical position before lowering the knee and placing the foot on the ground.

1. Body position and lifting action

2. Front- striking action.

3. Potential target area.

The return is very important as it removes the leg away from the aggressor, who may grab it. Returning the foot to the ground also stabilises the stance following the kick. Targeted areas are usually the groin, shin, navel or solar plexus. Higher areas can be targeted, however, they prolong the return to stability and balance may be compromised.

Mawashi geri (roundhouse kick)

The knee is raised and turned approximately 90˚; the leg is extended making contact with the side of the aggressor using either the ball or the top of the foot to perform the kick.

1. Lifting action.

2. Striking action.

3. Potential target area.

Yoko geri (side kick)

1. Body position and lifting action.

2. Side-striking action.

The weight of the body is placed on one foot pivoting in a 90° angle while simultaneously lifting the other leg. From this position the knee is kept at the same height and the lower leg is flicked forwards. The side of the foot makes contact with the target area, usually the knee, chest, stomach or groin.

3. Potential target area.

Ushiro geri (rear kick)

Straight

1. Body position and lifting action.

2. Back-kicking action.

The body weight is taken on one foot, while the other leg is raised and driven straight backwards. For a more powerful and accurate kick, pivot 90° before raising the other leg, then drive the foot backwards. The heel or the side of the foot is used to strike.

3. Potential target area.

Ushiro geri (rear kick)

Pivot style

1. Stance, with back to uke.

2. Pivoting action.

Tori's initial stance for this move is with her back to uke. She lifts her kicking leg and rotates her hips so that she pivots towards uke. She then kicks her leg out, straight through the target area.

3. Kicking action.

4. Pivoting action.

5. Kicking action and potential target area.

Fumi komi (stamp kick)

This is usually used for stamping on an aggressor's toes or instep, or is applied when an assailant is on the ground (possibly following a throw).

1. Stance and start of lifting action.

2. Continuation of lifting action.

3. Kicking action.

Tobe geri (flying kick)

There are various flying kicks, but although they are spectacular they require much practice and accuracy. If they are not performed correctly they are counter-productive.

1. Completion of flying kick.

2. Potential target area.

Standing

1. Tori's stance with back to uke.

2. Elbow action.

Empi uchi (elbow strike)

When using the elbow to strike, the palm of the hand should face the shoulder in order to prevent damage to the arm. Elbow strikes can be executed vertically or horizontally. Commonly the elbows are used when attacked from behind in a backwards and upwards motion to the stomach, or preferably the groin or ribs. The elbow can be driven downwards from above to target an assailant on the floor.

3. Potential target area.

Ground

1. Start of arm action.

2. Completion of arm action.

3. Potential target area.

1. Starting stance.

Hiza uchi (knee strike)

A knee strike is carried out simply by lifting the foot off the ground and bending the knee in one sharp action. The knees are commonly used to target the groin. They can also be used to devastating effect when the head is pulled forwards and impact is made with the knee to the face.

2. Lifting action.

3. Striking action.

Atama waza (head butt)

The head can be used as a striking tool; it can be applied in three directions: forwards, backwards and sideways. Tori's forehead is used for the forward strike, tori aims for uke's facial area (tori should avoid forehead-to-forehead contact).

1. Start of the waza action.

The backwards strike is when uke is behind tori and the back of the head is used. The side strike Is normally directed to the front of the head but the striking action involves an initial twisting of the neck.

2. Striking movement.

chapter 3:

Uke waza (blocking techniques)

Usually the forearms are used to deflect kicks and blows. By clenching the fists the muscles are tensed in the forearms. The forearm is used to block most hand attacks by rotating it upwards, and low hand attacks and kicks by rotating it downwards.

A jujitsuka encounters many situations and has to adapt to them. Blocking techniques are important because they serve to protect the body. There are many ways of blocking, as there are many situations that may arise. Once the basic principles of blocking are established, a jujitsuka can make subtle changes to adapt these blocks to the situation at hand. These techniques should be practised on the left as well as the right. To build up good technique and to prevent injury, always practise unfamiliar movements slowly and gradually increase the speed. With practice, confidence is built. Once a jujitsuka is proficient with these blocks they can be used in combination and in addition to striking and throwing techniques.

Nagashi uke (sweeping block)

This is probably the most frequently used block to a kick attack. Tori's stance should be with legs apart, one foot slightly in front of the other (in this instance, right foot in front of the left) with the knees slightly bent. Tori, keeping an open hand, rotates the hand and arm in an anti-clockwise direction and uses the palm to cup and/or push uke's attacking arm or leg away. Alternatively tori can keep hold of it and follow up with a throwing or striking technique of her own. Tori must use the palm of the hand for this technique as the fingers can become injured.

1. Start position.

2. Blocking action.

3. The full blocking action.

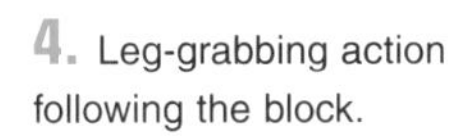

4. Leg-grabbing action following the block.

Gedan barai (downward block)

This block is used against attacks, usually kicks, to the solar plexus and abdomen area. Tori has her right foot in front of the left, with the knees slightly bent. Tori clenches her right fist (not too tightly) and swings her arm in a diagonal motion up and backwards. As the arm swings, the fist is turned in an anti-clockwise motion, from the initial thumb-upwards position to the back of the hand uppermost, with the little-finger side of the hand facing uke's arm or leg. It is important that if this is mastered on the right it is practised on the left. Most people are right-side dominant and therefore more likely to have to block with the left.

1. Starting position.

2. Hand and arm movement.

3. Blocking action.

Age uke (raising block)

This is a powerful block. It is used to prevent attacks to the chest, face and head region of the body. It requires precision and speed and therefore practice, to be effective. Tori has her right foot in front of her left, with the knees slightly bent. Tori clenches her right fist and drives it across her body, pushing it up and forwards simultaneously. The thrusting action should be derived from the hip. Tori rotates her right arm so that the back of it is facing her.

1. Starting position.

2. Hand and arm movement.

3. Blocking action.

Soto ude uke (outside forearm block)

This technique deflects attacks aimed at the centre of the body. Tori has her right foot in front of left, with the knees slightly bent. Tori clenches her fists, the right arm is bent at the elbow. The right elbow is lowered pushing the arm across tori's body to the left and rotated in a clockwise direction, turning the hand so that the knuckles are foremost.

1. Starting position.

2. Movement of the body.

3. Blocking action.

Ude barai (forearm sweeping block)

This block can have quite devastating effects. It is used against attacks aimed between the solar plexus and the lower region of the stomach. With practice the range of defence is increased. Tori has her left foot in front of her right, with the knees slightly bent. Tori has her left fist clenched and up and then clenches her right fist while trying to keep her shoulder relaxed. Tori pushes her right arm forwards in an aggressive movement, simultaneously rotating her right arm inwards (fist pointing down) and across her body. The power of the rotation is generated from the hips.

1. Starting position.

2. Movement of the body.

3. Blocking action.

Juji barai (cross block)

This blocking action is normally used for defence against a straight kick. The crossing of arms and making a fist strenghtens a blocking action. Once the block is successful, tori can grab uke's leg and counter with a kick. Alternatively, tori can push uke's leg to one side and perform a throw.

1. Starting position.

2. Arm and fist block.

3. Full blocking action.

Triangular grip break

The triangular grip break is a method used to break an aggressor's double lapel grip or front strangle. The fists, palms or entangled fingers are placed together in between the aggressor's arms and the arms are driven upwards to break the grip, following which, various options are open for tori to attack.

1. Stance and hand position.

2. Breaking the grip.

chapter 4:

Osaekomi waza (immobilisation)

The objective is to immobilise or hold and control the body with a joint lock, which limits ukes movement or chance of escape. Joint locks are used to achieve a holding action or to force a submission in training. It is also possible to incapacitate an assailant with joint dislocations.

Major joints that can be attacked to achieve immobilisation are the wrists and elbows (which tend to be somewhat stronger than the wrists). Knees and ankle joints are also vulnerable, as are the neck and spine. The level of force and speed applied will determine the amount of damage that can be inflicted. A ju jitsu move that is made too fast can result in permanent damage to a joint. In the case of the neck or spine an incorrect holding action could be fatal.

Kote waza
(wrist locks)

These grips are used to apply wrist locks. The wrist tends to be the weakest of all the joints when it comes to immobilisation. Once a grip is established, the wrist joint is attacked by rotating the hand against its natural range of movement. This creates pain and uke loses balance through endeavouring to reposition his body in a bid to stop the pain. A firm grip is essential for success.

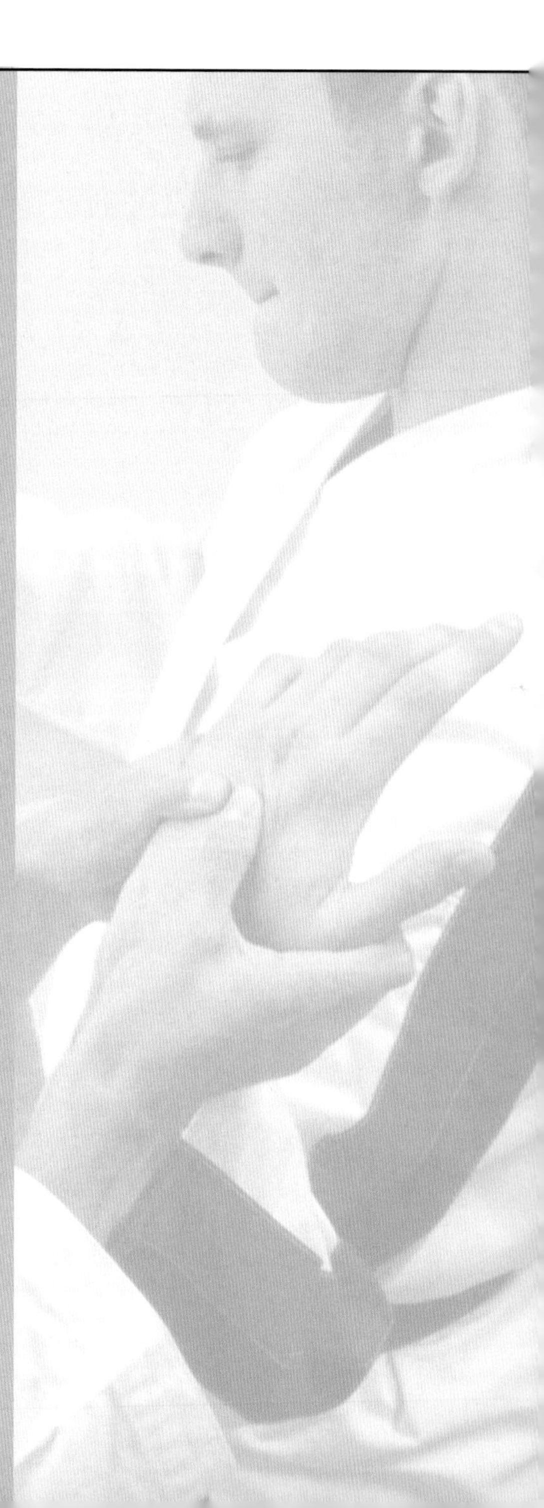

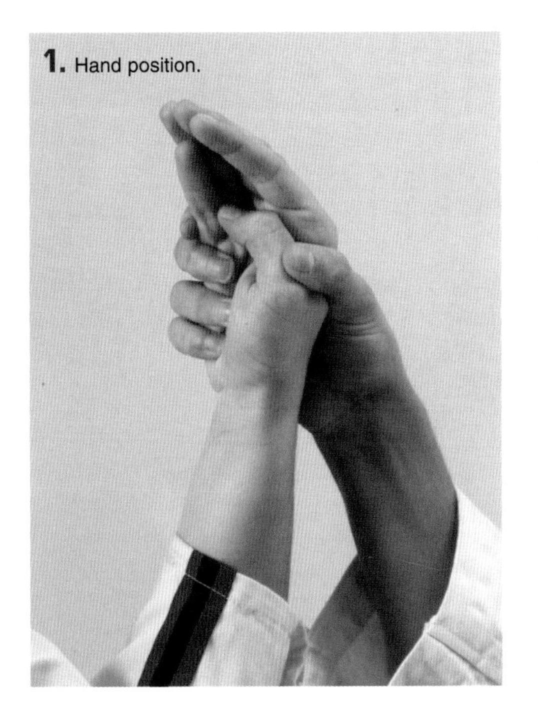

1. Hand position.

Back of the hand, thumb-to-thumb grasp

Tori grips uke's hand by placing her right thumb on the base of uke's thumb. Tori's fingers grip tightly round the rest of the hand to the little finger side of the hand. Tori twists uke's hand in a clockwise direction, pushing the hand towards the forearm. Pressure is exerted on the wrist joint. If tori continues the twisting action uke is forced face down to the ground. In this situation pressure is applied to the wrist using a twisting motion while continuing the pressure pushing uke's palm towards his own forearm.

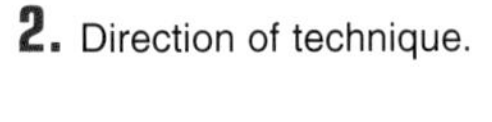

2. Direction of technique.

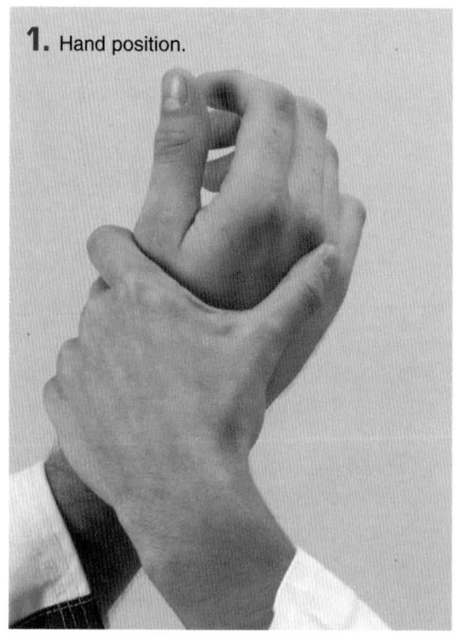

1. Hand position.

Thumb to the back of the hand

Tori grips uke's left hand with her right hand, the fingers grip around the base of uke's thumb and tori's thumb is placed on the back of uke's hand between where the third and forth fingers attach to the hand. Tori turns the wrist in a clockwise direction (however if this is done using the left hand against a right-handed aggressor, turn the wrist anti-clockwise). The pain will cause uke to flip on to his back. It is advisable to practise this on both sides, as it is likely that an aggressor will be right-handed, in which case the left hand will be needed for this technique.

2. Direction of technique.

Back of the hand grip inner thumb

Tori grips the base of uke's left thumb with her right thumb and wraps her fingers around the back of uke's hand. Tori keeps uke's hand in line with hers and twists the hand anti-clockwise to apply pressure to the wrist. This should also be practised using the left hand on uke's right hand, twisting in a clockwise direction.

1. Hand position.

2. Direction of technique.

Wrist lock with elbow

After uke grasps tori's wrist, tori makes a knife action with her hand, rotates her wrist, aiming the strike at uke's little finger, and grabs uke's wrist. Tori continues the movement until uke's hand and arm are behind uke's back. Push towards the shoulder blades.

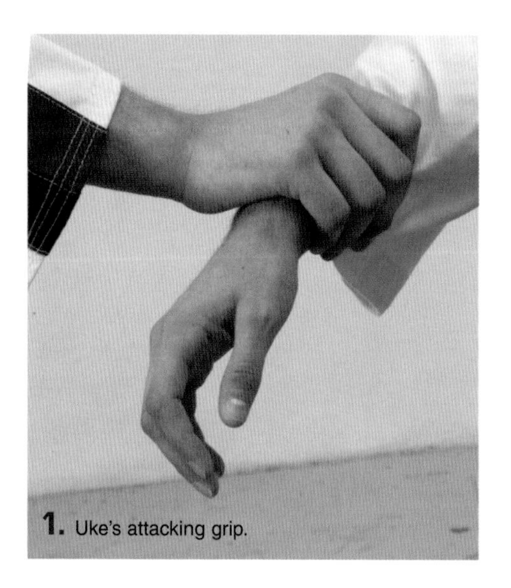

1. Uke's attacking grip.

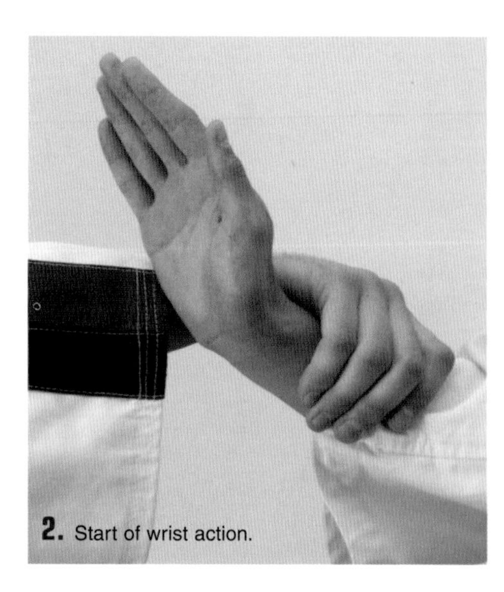

2. Start of wrist action.

3. Continuation of tori's grip.

4. Arm grip and direction of wrist.

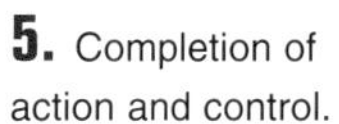

5. Completion of action and control.

Wrist lock from a wrist grab

Uke grabs tori's wrist with her right hand. The grip would be fingers over the wrist. Tori does a knife action with her hand and rotates her wrist, aiming for uke's little finger to touch uke's wrist. Tori continues rotation of her own wrist after gripping uke's wrist with her other hand placed on uke's elbow joint. Uke is taken down to the ground with a half-circle action.

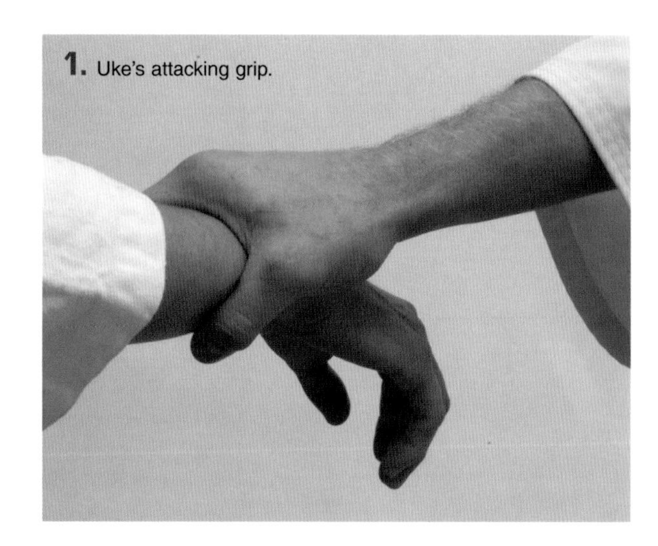

1. Uke's attacking grip.

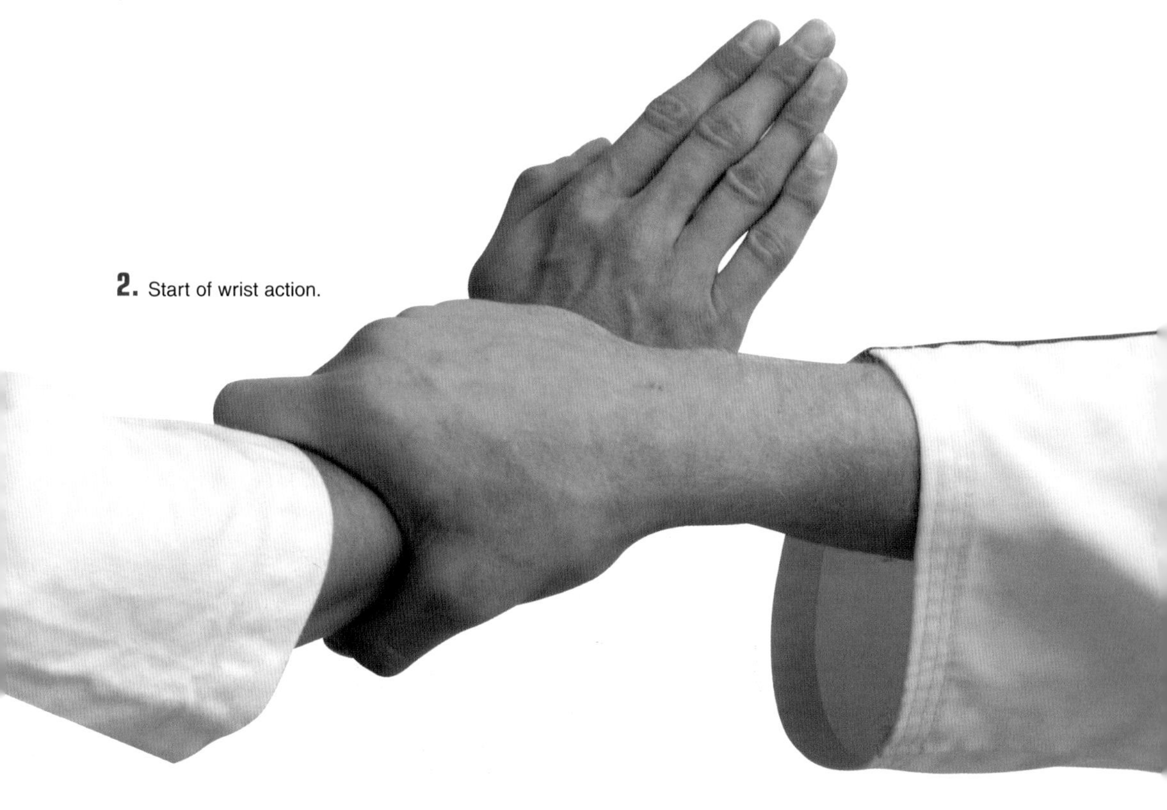

2. Start of wrist action.

3. Tori's elbow grip.

4. Completion of action.

Kote dori (Wrist trap)

With uke and tori both facing forwards, tori slightly behind uke, tori slides his right arm through the gap under uke's armpit. Using his left hand, tori bends uke's arm and simultaneously grasps the back of uke's hand with his right hand. This is an immobilisation move often used by the police. The pressure on the wrist can be increased by pushing uke's hand down towards uke's own forearm.

Starting positions.

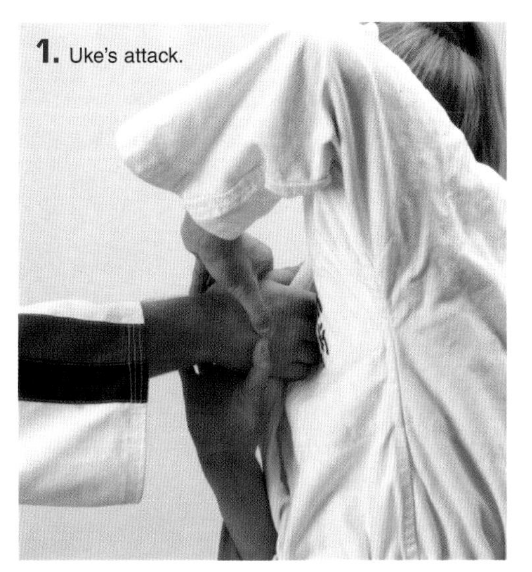

1. Uke's attack.

Ura kote (reverse wrist lock)

This is usually used when an attacker grabs clothing in the chest area. Tori catches hold of uke's right grasping hand with both hands, with her fingers around uke's wrist and her thumbs on the back of uke's hand, then twists the hand in a clockwise direction. Uke's hand is pushed towards his own forearm. This will usually cause uke to bend away from the pain, allowing him to be thrown.

2. Direction of wrist rotation.

Kote gaeshi (wrist reverse)

Uke has gripped, or is attempting to grip, the front of tori's jacket or clothing with his right hand. Tori grasps the hand with her thumbs pressing into the back of the hand and pushes it to uke's rear. Uke is forced to the ground. If done abruptly the wrist may be broken.

1. Uke's attacking grip.

2. Direction of wrist rotation.

Wrist grab attack

Uke grabs tori by the wrist. Tori has the option to break away or to turn it to his own advantage.

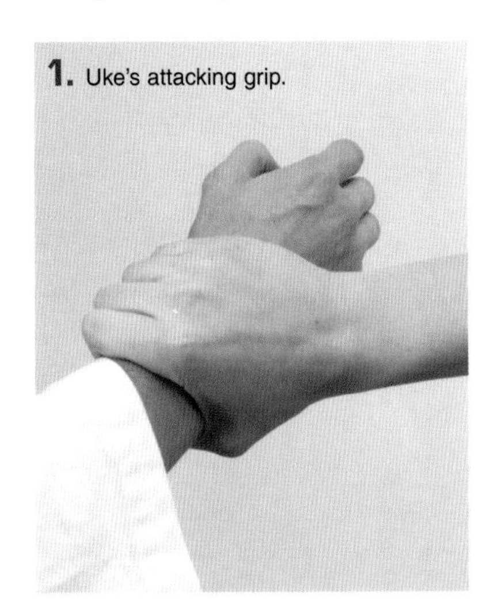

1. Uke's attacking grip.

2. Initial action.

3. Full breaking of grip.

Kansetsu waza (armlocks)

An effective arm lock is applied to the elbow in these techniques. The moves also rely on a wrist lock, from which more pressure is applied. Tori uses various parts of his or her body as a lever base.

Ude gatame (straight armlock)

Tori grasps uke's arm at the wrist and turns the arm so the wrist is pointing upwards. Tori takes her other hand over uke's arm and under uke's elbow, placing her hand on top of uke's forearm to create a pivot to apply pressure. This can be done while on the inside or outside of uke's arms.

1. Position for inside armlock.

2. Position for outside armlock.

Eri gatame (collar hold)

From a standing position to uke's right side, tori grabs uke's right wrist. Tori's fingers clasp the inner wrist and twist the arm in an anti-clockwise direction. At the same time, tori places her left arm under uke's armpit and grabs the opposite collar with the fingers inside the jacket. Pressure is applied to uke's elbow joint with a twisting action applied to uke's right arm.

Ashi gatame (leg armlock)

Tori has control of uke's body with do jime (scissor action of the legs). He releases this grip and one leg swings over uke's arm, which is held by tori. Tori uses the other leg to push uke's support knee away, collapsing uke's body. The arm lock is applied by pulling against the elbow joint. This is accomplished by pulling up with the wrist grip.

Hiza gatame (knee armlock)

Tori has control of uke's body with do jime (scissor action of the legs). He releases this grip and one leg swings over uke's arm, which is held by tori. Tori uses the other leg to push uke's support knee away, collapsing uke's body. The arm lock is applied by tori placing the knee against the elbow joint.

Waki gatame (armpit lock)

Uke cross-grips tori's wrist. Tori takes her gripped arm backwards. Rotating her wrists to take uke's arm, she then places her armpit on uke's elbow.

Ashi kansetsu waza (leg locks)

The objective of leg locks is, in the first instance, to apply pressure against the weakest joint, which tends to be the knee. As with locks to any other joint, precise positioning is necessary to apply a technique successfully. Not all leg locks apply pressure to the knee or ankle joints, some cause immense pain to the leg muscles.

Hiza hishigi (knee crush or dislocation)

There are several ways to apply this lock.

1. With uke flat on his face. Tori uses her left hand to grasp uke's heel and pushes it into the inner knee joint of uke's other knee. Tori immediately uses her right hand to grasp uke's left instep and bends uke's leg back, pushing uke's heel towards uke's own buttocks. As uke's right foot is in the joint, the strain is placed on the left knee joint.

2. Again with uke flat on his face, tori places her own lower leg in the groove of uke's knee joint. Using her right hand and chest, if need be, tori pushes uke's lower leg, closing down the gap between uke's heel and buttocks.

Kata ashi hishigi (single-leg crush or dislocation)

This same technique can be applied from three different positions, but the result is the same.

1. Tori standing. When uke is on his back, tori stands in front of him, by his feet. The technique is easier to execute if tori is slightly to one side. So tori steps to her left and traps uke's right ankle under her armpit, squeezing tight and securing the position by taking her right arm under uke's leg and clenching her other hand for support. Tori bends backwards while maintaining a strong grip of uke's leg and pressing her forearm into uke's lower leg or calf region, using her body weight to apply pressure to the ankle joint. The effectiveness of the lock can be increased by pushing sideways.

2. Tori in a seated position. This technique can be applied with the same grip of uke's leg under tori's armpit, but this time tori is in a seated position supporting herself with her right leg. Her left leg is stretched diagonally across uke's abdomen. Tori then leans backwards. Alternatively, to apply the lock to the knee joint, tori squeezes her knees to clamp uke's leg tight, and instead of leaning directly backwards, tori leans to the left and pushes inwards with her left knee pressing on uke's outer knee.

3. Uke flat on front; tori standing. Another single leg lock can be applied. This method is used either when uke is lying flat on his stomach or as a continuation from the first version described above when uke struggles. While maintaining the grip on uke's leg, tori steps her left leg over uke's held leg. Uke has no choice but to turn on to her front. Tori bends her knees to give herself a solid base and then leans backwards applying pressure to uke's leg.

Ryo ashi hishigi (double-leg crush or dislocation)

This technique is very similar to kata ashi hishigi, only this time both legs are trapped and locked. It also can be applied in a variety of positions.

1. Tori standing. When uke is on his back, tori stands in front of him by his feet. Tori traps both of uke's legs at the ankle by placing them under her armpits. Tori squeezes tightly and secures the position by taking her arms under uke's legs and grasping her hands together for support. Tori bends backwards while maintaining a strong grip of uke's legs and pressing her forearms into the calf regions of uke's legs, using her body-weight to apply pressure to the ankle joints.

2. Tori in a seated position. As with the first technique, tori grips round the outside of both uke's legs and clasps her hands together in the middle. Tori wraps both legs around uke's legs and crosses them at the ankles. Tori then leans backwards. Tori does not fall backwards to the mat or ground because she is counter-balanced by uke's weight.

3. Uke flat on front, tori standing. The double-leg lock can be applied when uke is lying flat on his stomach or as a continuation from the first version described above when uke struggles. While maintaining the grip on uke's legs, tori steps her right leg over uke's legs, twisting uke over as she does so. Uke has no choice but to turn on to his front. Tori bends her knees to give herself a solid base and then leans backwards applying pressure to uke's legs. This technique, if adjusted, can also be a spine lock. To convert it into a spine lock tori, while maintaining the grip on the legs, bends uke backwards and pushes her weight down on to uke's back. Spine damage will occur.

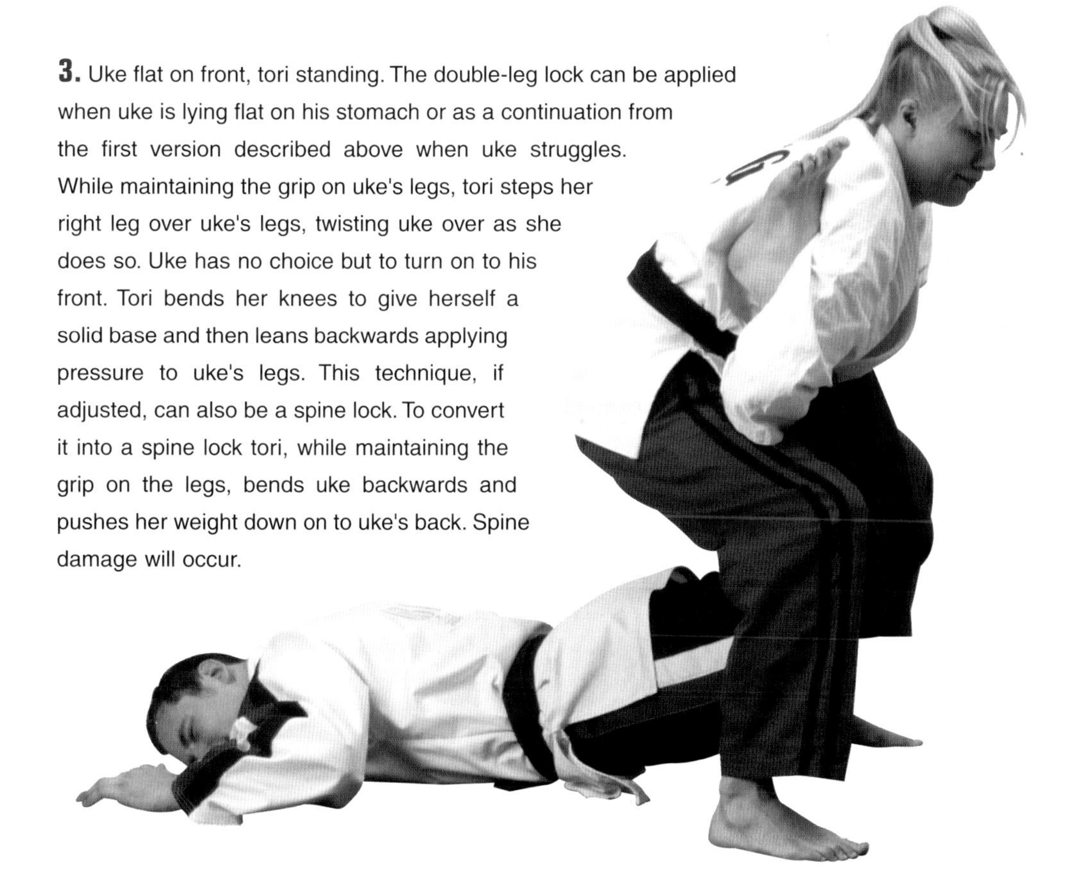

Ashi kannuki (leg bolt lock)

Tori is lying on her back with uke transversally on top (chest to chest). Tori traps uke's right leg by entangling her right leg around uke's leg and hooking his instep under her own left lower leg. Tori then pushes the toes of the left foot upwards, trapping the top of uke's foot. Tori pulls uke's body in tight and straightens her legs to apply the lock.

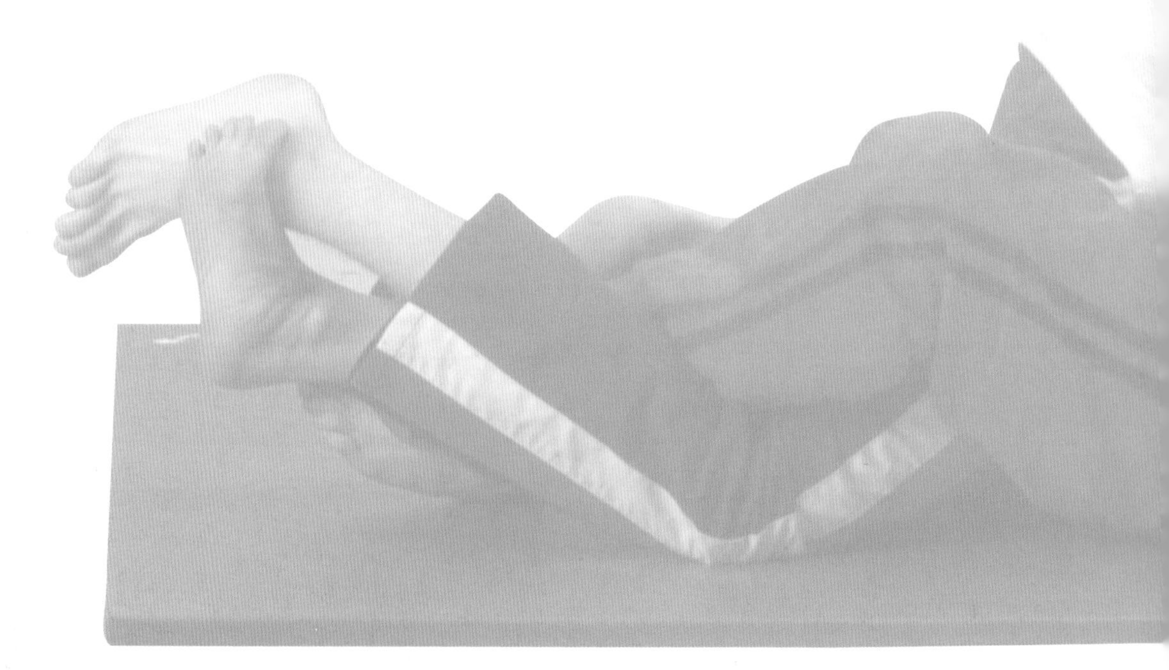

Kubi kansetsu waza (spine locks)

These techniques are potentially the most dangerous in ju jitsu, the aim being to twist the neck where it meets the spine. The moves can be used to immobilise an opponent when fighting on the ground. and can be fatal if applied incorrectly.

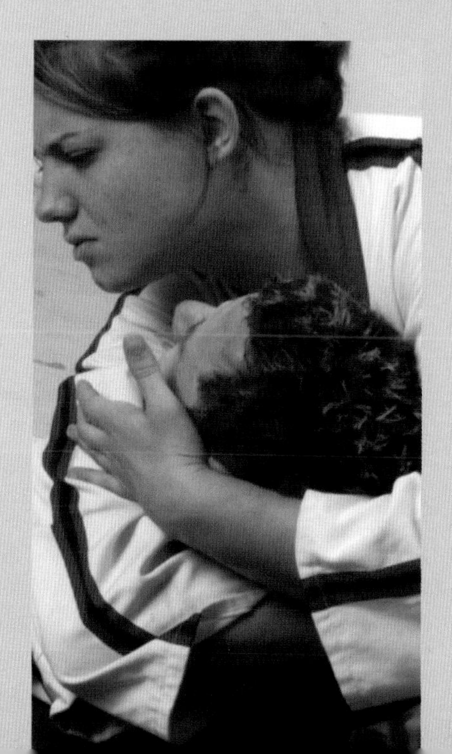

Kubi hishigi (dislocation neck lock/neck crush)

Uke is on his back, tori sits astride uke with one or both knees on the ground. Tori sits on uke's chest towards her head. Tori places one hand over the other on to the back of uke's head and pulls uke's head forwards. Increased pressure is added by taking the head to one side while maintaining the forwards pressure.

Oase hishigi (dislocation in immobilisation)

Uke is on her back, tori sits astride uke with either one or both knees on the ground. Tori supports himself with his left arm and leans forwards, moving his head towards uke's right shoulder. Tori then slides his right arm under uke's neck and bends his arm backwards to grip his own belt (so that the back of tori's hand makes contact with tori's own hip area as he grasps the belt). Uke's head is clamped under tori's armpit, tori pushes against the mat with his left hand and bends to his back right corner.

Kesa gatame kubi hishigi (scarf hold neck dislocation)

Tori holds uke with a kesa gatarme (scarf hold). Sitting next to uke, tori puts her right arm round uke's head and traps uke's right arm under her left armpit with legs spread wide. While maintaining the arm around the head, tori clasps her hands together. Tori bends forward locking uke's head between her right arm and right upper chest, and uke's head is forced to the left

Atama hishigi (head crush)

Uke is lying flat on his back. Tori sits next to uke and wraps her right arm around uke's head. Tori clasps her hands together and squeezes uke's head using the cutting edge of the forearm to press against uke's face. This is painful in itself, but to increase the effectiveness tori can lean backwards which draws the head up and puts pressure on the neck, applying a neck lock.

Kuzure kesa kubi hishigi (broken scarf hold neck crush)

Uke is on her back. Tori sits next to uke, places uke's arm under his left armpit and squeezes tight. As uke tries to sit up, tori places his right arm behind uke's neck and under uke's left armpit. Pressure is applied to uke's neck when tori leans backwards.

Tate hishigi (standing neck crush)

Uke is standing. This works best against an uke with a bent-over posture. Tori puts his right arm over uke's head, so that uke's head is in tori's right armpit. Tori's right forearm goes across uke's throat and tori links his hands together. To perform a strangle, tori pulls his forearm up into the throat, or to apply the neck lock tori leans back, twisting sideways and upwards.

chapter 5:

Defence against attacks

This chapter looks at various attacking actions from an opponent and shows a number of ways in which they can be countered using throws (nage waza), striking techniques (atemi waza), strangle techniques (shimi waza), and joint locks (kam setsu waza).

Gan men tsuki (punch to the face)

In this instance the aggressor (uke) is in front of tori and throws a punch to the face. All of the techniques presented require, in the first instance, a standard atemi waza block to the inside of uke's arm action (see pages 28–55)

Possible responses

Tai otoshi (body drop)

Tori requires an upright posture in a preparation stance, one leg slightly forward. As uke swings the punch, tori blocks. The blocking arm immediately bends at the wrist and takes uke's forearm or cloth in that region, if available, and pulls in a semi-circular action. At the same time tori swings her left leg back, which rotates her body and shoulders. Tori places her other arm around uke's head and rotates uke's body over her right leg, which is blocking uke's right leg. This action uses uke's momentum from the throwing of the punch. If tori maintains the grip on uke's arm she can pull down so that uke ends on his face and ude gatame (arm lock) is applied.

1. Starting position.

2. Blocking action.

3. Gripping action.

4. Rotation entry.

5. Throwing position.

6. Direction of throw.

Osoto otoshi (major outer drop)

Tori blocks the punching arm, simultaneously stepping forward with her left foot. The heel of her hand is driven into uke's chin or nose (specific targets) or facial area. This forces uke's head back. Simultaneously tori steps behind uke's right leg, placing the sole of the foot on the ground in between uke's legs.

1. Starting position.

2. Blocking position.

3. Gripping position.

The drive of tori's hand could push uke's head with varying force into the ground. This would certainly render him unconscious and could, depending on the force, administer a fractured skull and/or kill him. To go into disorientation mode once uke is off-balance, tori releases the face attack. Uke will wind himself as he lands on his back. To assist on this control, the blocking arm, if possible, should hold uke's arm.

4. Start of striking action.

5. Throwing action.

Harai goshi (sweeping hip)

Uke throws a punch. Tori blocks and swings her left leg behind her, which rotates her body, while simultaneously grasping the back of uke's neck with her inside forearm. The blocking arm then grips uke's throwing arm and pulls uke on to her so there is complete body contact. Tori then leans forwards which tends to bring uke's weight on to his toes. Tori stands on her left foot and sweeps the back of her thigh on to the front of uke's thigh and rotates. To achieve maximum effect, tori lets uke go completely and the height from which uke falls completely winds him. Tori then follows through with an atemi waza (see page 28–55).

1. Starting position.

2. Blocking position.

3. Gripping position.

4. Start of throw.

5. Full throwing action.

Ago tsuki (upper cut)

Tori blocks uke's punch and swings into an upper cut. When executing the upper cut the wrist is launched from the waist level. Tori can target the point on the chin if uke's stance is upright, but quite often the mechanics of the thrown punch have uke leaning forwards, so the target of the punch is then the throat.

1. Starting position.

2. Blocking position.

3. Target position of punch.

Shuto uchi (hand knife edge strike)

Tori blocks on the inside, parrying uke's arm outwards, and creating a knife-edge with her other hand, with the knuckles facing down. Tori aims for the side of uke's neck, a nerve area which is situated approximately 5cm (2in) down from uke's earlobe. This blow can also hit the carotid artery. On the secondary movement tori aims for the other side of the neck; the target area is closer to the windpipe following the block. Tori positions her body at 45° to strike the other side of neck.

1. Starting position.

2. Blocking position.

3. Striking action.

4. Target strike area.

Avoidance using an outside block

The following techniques use a different principle, avoidance of the initial attack, rather than just blocking and attacking. Tori steps back and applies forearm blocks to the outside of the thrown punch. This action tends to over-extend uke's punching arm rather than block it.

Choku zuki (straight punch)

1. Start position.

2. Blocking action.

Avoid the punch. Uke's arm is pushed across her body and the other arm punches into the floating rib area.

3. Target punch area.

Osoto gari (major outer sweep)

Avoidance block. Uke steps forwards with his right leg as the right arm slides from the block across uke's face and the hand is placed on the shoulder. Tori steps behind and leans forwards simultaneously pulling uke's head back. She then sweeps with her leg.

1. Starting position.

2. Blocking action.

3. Start of stepping action.

4. Continuation of stepping action.

5. Sweeping action.

Gyaku ogoshi (reverse major hip throw)

Tori avoids the punch and blocks to the outside. Tori's arm goes around uke's head and tori steps behind uke, placing the rear of her hip into uke's back and throwing him over her hips.

1. Starting position.

2. Blocking action.

3. Start of stepping action.

4. Placement of hip.

5. Lifting action.

6. Full throwing action.

Gyaku uki otoshi (reverse floating drop)

1. Starting position.

2. Blocking action.

3. Stepping to uke's rear.

4. Body position.

Avoidance block. Tori steps around behind uke placing her arm on uke's shoulder, preferably grabbing cloth if any is available. Tori grabs the opposite shoulder, simultaneously using the hand of the blocking arm to grip the other shoulder. Tori quickly runs backwards maybe one or two steps and goes down on to one knee. Uke's back should be in a full arch.

5. Throwing action.

Gyaku morote gari (reverse double-leg grab)

Tori avoids with an outside block. She then steps behind and immediately grabs the front of uke's shins, at the same time using her shoulders or head to push into uke's back or buttocks. This tips uke forward and uke's legs are scooped away. This can be followed up with ashi garame (entangled leg armlock).

1. Starting position.

2. Blocking action and body position.

3. Stepping action.

4. Gripping action.

5. Full throwing action.

Hadaku jime (naked strangle)

This strangle is executed in a standing position. It is tori's objective to get behind uke. Following the attack, a punch is thrown, tori blocks and moves behind uke while positioning her forearm against uke's throat. Tori clasps her hands and places her shoulder against the back of uke's neck. Then she steps back, forcing uke off balance, and exerts pressure on uke's shoulder with her arm. This either controls uke or, within 10 to 15 seconds, uke becomes unconscious. A longer timespan could result in death due to a lack of oxygen to the brain.

1. Starting position.

2. Blocking position.

3. Step pattern for body and hand positioning.

4. The full action.

Uranage (rear throw)

Tori avoids the initial attack, pushes across and steps around behind uke, grasping both arms around uke's waist. Tori bends her knees, dropping her waist below uke's. Tori pulls uke's body towards her to make contact and lift uke by straightening the legs. Tori simultaneously rotates, throwing uke over her left or right shoulder depending on where tori's head is. Tori aims to throw uke on to his shoulder or head.

1. Starting position.

2. Blocking and body position.

3. Step pattern for body and hand positioning.

4. Start of lifting action.

5. Continuation of lifting action.

6. Full throwing action.

Shuto uchi (hand knife-edge strike)

Avoiding the punch with a block using the lower forearm, tori delivers a blow to the side of uke's neck using a knife hand.

1. Starting position.

2. Blocking position.

3. Step pattern for body position.

4. Start of striking action.

5. Target strike and arm control.

Ude gatame (armlock)

Tori avoids the attack with a block. The blocking arm slides down uke's arm until tori can grasp uke's wrist. Tori's other arm transfers over and the palm of the hand is placed on uke's elbow. Simultaneously tori pulls uke's arm with the wrist grip and circling with her arm and uke's body gradually getting the arm lower to the ground until uke is flat on his face. Tori could then stay in position and immobilise or kneel on the arm pulling back on wrist and arm will break.

1. Starting position.

2. Blocking position.

3. Start of hand control.

4. Continuation of hand control.

5. Tori's body position.

6. Start of arm control.

7. Continuation of arm control.

8. Completion of technique.

Morote gari (double-leg grab)

Avoidance of the punch is achieved by ducking. Tori avoids the punch completely by suddenly bending her knees and stepping forwards, using the top of her head or shoulder to charge forwards into the stomach of uke. Tori grips both uke's legs behind the knees and scoops the legs towards tori as uke loses his balance from a head butt or shoulder barge.

1. Starting position.

2. Avoidance of punching action.

3. Gripping action.

4. Throwing action.

Punch to the stomach

Uke aims a punch at tori's solar plexus muscle group. This punch is launched in a screwing action from uke's waist level. Tori's initial response is to block the punch.

Sumi otoshi (floating drop)

Tori blocks the front punch with gedan barai (downward block) and at same time steps towards uke's side. Tori's other hand is placed at the side of uke's head. Tori's blocking arm wraps down and around uke's punching arm and pushes the head sideways as hard as possible. This pins uke's weight on to his right foot and throws uke to the ground. This is a complete hand throw: none of tori's body makes contact.

1. Starting position.

2. Blocking action.

3. Stepping action.

4. Throwing action.

Atama waza (head butt)

Tori blocks the punch, parrying the hand outwards. Tori then closes down the space and uses her forehead to strike the front of uke's face directly on the nose or above it (bridge). Tori can make the attack stronger by simultaneously grasping the back of uke's head (neck) and pulling her head forwards simultaneously as tori's head is coming forwards. Tori must be accurate using her forehead, otherwise tori could herself be knocked out!

1. Starting position.

2. Blocking action.

3. Gripping action.

4. Head action.

5. Completion of technique.

Attack with single-lapel grab

An initial grab attack starts with one hand first. The object of the series of responses is to attack before the other hand also grabs or a possible blow is attempted. The surprise element is very much a part of the response to the initial one-hand lapel grab.

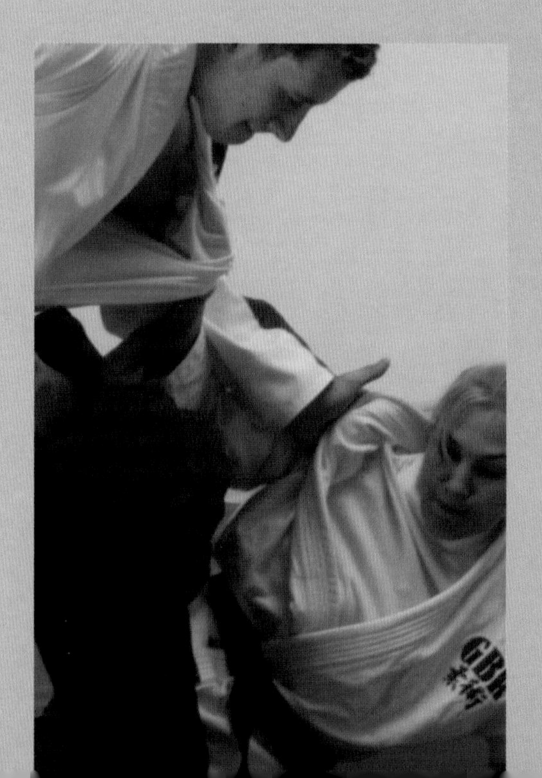

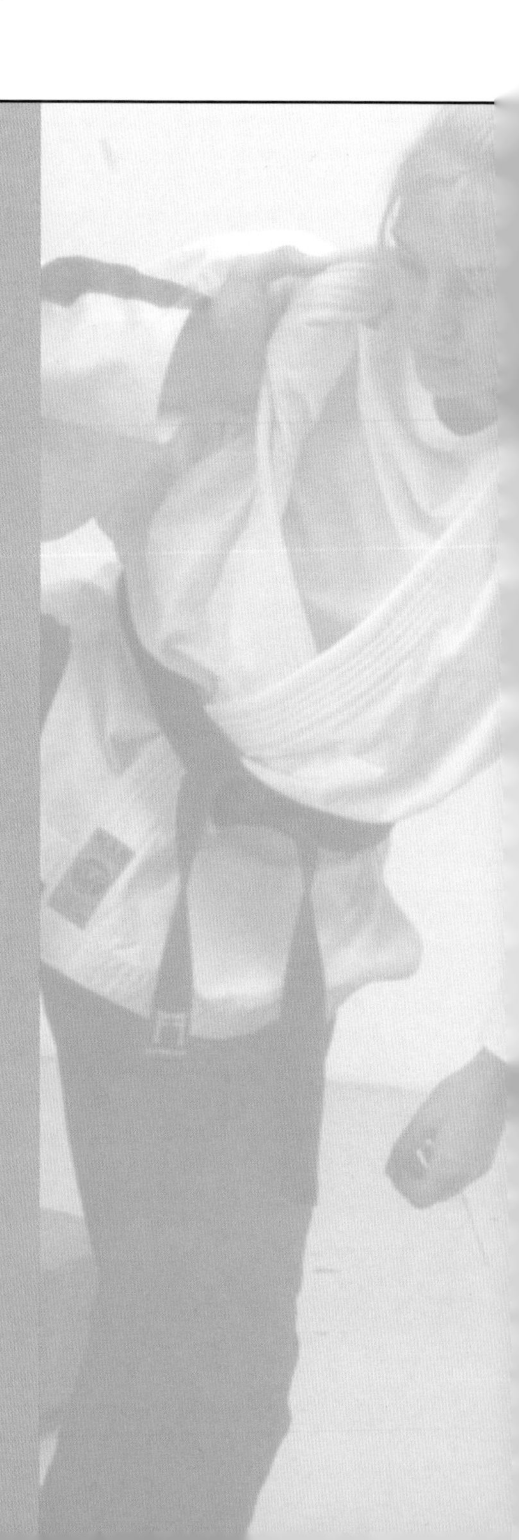

Possible responses

Kani basami (leg scissors)

Tori grips uke's left lapel with her right hand. Tori jumps into position, placing her right leg across the front of uke's thighs and the left leg behind the knees or calf region. Tori then pushes back with her right leg and forwards with the left, hence the basami or scissors part of the name. Uke falls to his rear.

1. Tori attacking initial lapel grab.

2. Continuation of leg attack.

3. Completion of the technique.

Kani garami (crab entanglement)

Tori attempts kani basami, but as tori does so uke resists by leaning forwards. In response, tori changes the direction of rotation (rolling in a clockwise direction). The front of tori's left leg pushes uke's ankles or shins and the back of tori's right leg pushes uke's knees at the back. In this instance uke falls on to his front.

1. Initial cross-lapel grab

2. First leg attacking position.

3. Second leg attacking position.

4. Completion of throw.

Attack with double-lapel grip

From in front of tori, uke grips the lapels or cloth with both hands. This is a common initial attack from uke, which initially is used to control tori. It can then develop into a head butt or push. If the attacker is very skilled, there are many throws that can be attempted from this grip.

Possible responses

Hiza strike (knee strike)

1. Uke's double-lapel grip.

Tori brings the knee sharply up into uke's groin area. If uke's stance is slightly to one side, the knee strike could be to the front of the thigh, which can numb the leg.

2. Tori's initial gripping response.

3. Completion of action.

Kosoto gake (minor outer hook)

The heel of the hand strikes uke's chin with the fingers in the facial area. Tori simultaneously hooks her right leg behind uke's knee, pushing the head back as hard as possible, following through down to the ground.

1. Uke's double-lapel grip.

2. Tori's initial step and hand attack.

3. Hand and leg contact.

4. Completion of throw.

The triangular grip break

The triangle grip break consists of breaking the double lapel grip by placing the fists together or palms together or entangled finger grip and driving the arms upwards. The following techniques can be used following this break.

Atama waza (head butt)

Uke grips tori's lapels. Tori's immediate reaction is to head butt uke to the face. This is a stronger technique if tori grabs the back of uke's head and pulls towards her.

1. Uke's double-lapel grip.

2. Tori's hand positioning.

3. Head action.

4. Completion of technique.

Ippon seoi nage (one arm shoulder throw)

Tori grabs one wrist on the outside and, with the other hand, makes a knife position, taking it over uke's forearm and under the other forearm while simultaneously swinging his leg behind him and rotating his body pushing his hips across. Tori's arm will end up under uke's opposite arm. Tori bends her knees and pulls uke forwards, to straighten her legs, and rotating simultaneously.

1. Uke's double-lapel grip.

2. Tori's first action.

3. Attacking through uke's arms.

4. Body positioning.

5. Rotating through hips.

6. Completion of throw.

Okuriashi barai (double-foot sweep)

Tori can mirror uke's double lapel grip by doing the same action or holding uke's upper arm area with both hands. Tori then steps back and pulls uke forward and up on to his toes. With either foot, although right-handed fighters tend to use their right foot, the sole of tori's foot is used to sweep both of uke's feet away in a sideways action.

1. Uke's double-lapel grip.

2. Tori's responding grip.

3. Start of step pattern.

4. Full body contact.

5. Completion of technique.

Sasae tsurikomi ashi (propping drawing ankle)

Using a triangle grip break, tori immediately wraps uke's right arm with tori's left arm, simultaneously stepping to the side and blocking the front of uke's foot as uke steps forwards. Tori's other arm comes up under uke's armpit. The pulling action is over tori's left shoulder. To make the fall extremely heavy, tori falls on top of uke's chest (ribcage).

1. Uke's double-lapel grip.

2. Breaking uke's grip.

3. Tori's grip on uke's arm.

4. Stepping into body contact.

5. Completion of throw.

Koshi guruma (hip wheel)

Tori makes a triangle break, wraps her arm around uke's right hand and simultaneously grasps uke's head with a rear neck grab, wheeling uke over her hips. To make the fall extremely heavy, tori falls on top of uke.

1. Uke's double-lapel grip.

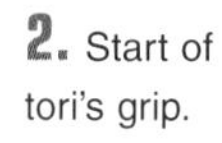

2. Start of tori's grip.

3. Start of hip rotation.

4. Continuation of hip rotation.

5. Throwing action.

Tomoe nage (circular throw)

Grabbing hold of uke's clothes or arms, tori suddenly drops on to her back. This action pulls uke forward. Tori can then place her right foot in uke's stomach. A rotating action is required to take uke either on to his back or side and to ensure that uke does not land on tori.

1. Uke's double-lapel grip.

2. Start of tori's grip.

3. Start of stepping action.

4. Falling action.

5. Lifting action.

6. Throwing action.

1. Uke's double-lapel grip.

Sumi gaeshi (corner throw)

This is the same throwing motion as the previous throw, except here tori places the instep of her foot into the groin area before using the rotating action to take uke either on to his back or side and to ensure that uke does not land on tori.

2. Start of tori's grip.

3. Tori's foot position.

4. Falling action.

5. Throwing action.

Yoko guruma (side wheel)

Tori throws her body on to the ground slightly sideways, blocking the front of uke's shins with her body. This sudden drop takes uke off balance and tori does a wheeling action with her hands to take tori over.

1. Uke's double-lapel grip.

2. Start of tori's grip.

3. Stepping action.

4. Falling action.

5. Throwing action.

1. Uke's double-lapel grip.

Morote shuto uchi (double handed knife-edge strike)

Using a triangle escape, at the height of the break tori makes shuto te (knife hand) and brings it sharply down on to the collar bone or shoulder area. This can numb uke's arms.

2. Breaking the grip.

3. Triangular action.

4. Hand strike to target area.

Kick to the groin

1. Uke's double-lapel grip.

2. Tori's initial step away.

This is normally a one-step action. Tori touches the advanced foot with the sole of her front foot which, to be effective, uke must believe to be a side-sweep attack. Uke steps back and, simultaneously, tori pulls forward and places the sweeping leg into uke's stomach. Tori drops on to his back, taking uke over in a full circle.

3. Start of kicking action.

4. Completion of kicking action.

Ear slap

1. Uke's double-lapel grip.

Using a triangle break, tori takes the arms in a half-circle action outwards and cups her hands, ear slaps both uke's ears. This can burst eardrums and has excellent disorientation repercussions.

2. Breaking action.

3. Slapping action.

1. Uke's double-lapel grip.

Wrist lock into waki gatame

Tori secures uke's wrist to her own chest with one hand. She then reaches across and grips uke's opposite elbow turning in a circular motion, rotating the wrist and reaching the arm over uke's arm so that uke's arm is in tori's armpit and pulling uke in a semi circle. This forces uke down to the ground using his armpit as the fulcrum for the armlock.

2. Tori's initial action.

3. Continuation of action,

4. Tori's hand position.

5. Continuation of hand position.

6. Completion of the technique.

Grab from behind

A major attacking move can be made from behind. When uke attacks tori in this way by surprise, the objective is to immobilise tori's arms or body. The head is controlled by a neck hold or attempted strangle.Tori can respond with either throws or strikes.

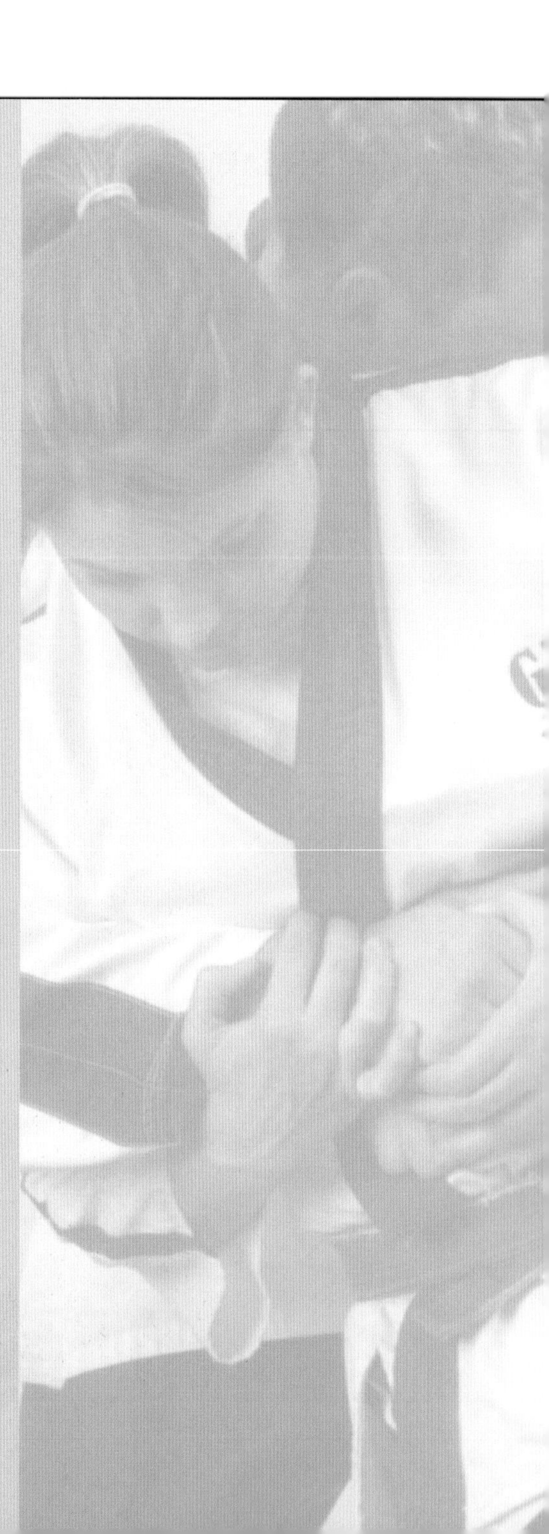

Possible responses

Gyaku atama waza (reverse head butt)

Tori pushes her chin down to her chest and snaps her back head very fast into uke's nose.

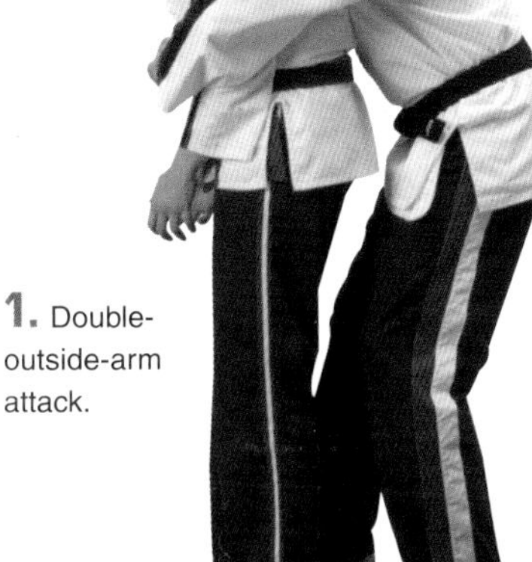

1. Double-outside-arm attack.

2. Start of head action.

3. Completion of head action.

Ashi dori (leg grab)

Tori leans forwards and grips one of uke's legs, pulling the leg through her own legs and falling backwards, aiming to sit on uke's stomach. This will wind uke.

1. Double-outside-arm attack.

2. Start of body action.

3. Hand placement.

4. Lifting action.

5. Completion of throw.

1. Double-outside-arm attack.

Tai otoshi uchi makikomi (body drop inner winding throw)

Tori rotates her body while simultaneously falling forward on to the ground. The objective is for tori's back to land on top of uke's chest. This will cause serious damage to the ribs and back.

2. Tori's hand action.

3. Side-stepping action.

4. Completion of throw.

Ippon seoi nage (one-arm shoulder throw)

Tori breaks uke's grip by driving her arm up sideways, then reaches across with both hands and takes both of uke's arms. Tori bends her knees and rotates her shoulders, taking uke sideways or directly over the top of tori's shoulder onto his head and back

1. Double-outside-arm attack.

2. Grip-breaking action.

3. Tori's hand position.

4. Start of lifting action.

5. Continuation of lifting action.

6. Throwing action.

Katsugi gatame (shoulder carry armlock)

Tori breaks uke's grip by lifting her arm sideways. She reaches across and takes a two-handed grip on uke's wrist. Rotating the wrist so the inside of uke's elbow is facing upwards, tori then uses her own shoulder as a fulcrum to apply pressure.

If done fast, the arm will break.

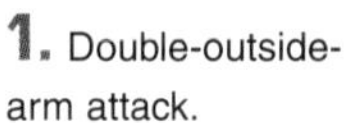

1. Double-outside-arm attack.

2. Grip-breaking action.

3. Tori's hand position.

4. Start of arm control.

5. Completion of technique.

Gyaku empi uchi (reverse elbow strike)

Tori breaks uke's grip by lifting the arms. The mechanics of the elbow strike require tori to make a fist, then push the arm out straight and bring the elbow and fist backwards together, finishing with the fist as close to her own shoulder as possible.

1. Double-outside-arm attack.

2. Grip-breaking action.

3. Step

4. Elbow strike

Grab around the waist

Uke grabs tori around the waist from behind. As with the grab around the arms, tori has her back to uke. The grip occurs when tori's arms are not close to her body.

1. Double-outside-arm waist attack.

Fumi komi (stamping kick)

Tori uses the heel to strike directly down on top of uke's foot, this can then be followed with a second technique such as makikomi (winding throw) or an empi uchi (elbow strike).

2. Lifting action.

3. Stamping action.

Harai makikomi (winding sweeping hip)

Tori reaches across and takes uke's wrist, simultaneously moving her leg to the outside of uke's right leg. Tori leans forwards and starts to rotate, which brings uke up on to his toes. Tori then makes a sweeping action with her outside leg.

1. Double-outside-arm waist attack.

2. Tori's hand and arm position.

3. Tori's hand and leg position.

4. Completion of throw.

Gyaku empi uchi (reverse elbow strike)

Tori leans forwards to create distance between her back and uke's front. Tori then twists the upper body, simultaneously taking the elbow back into uke's throat or neck.

1. Double-outside-arm waist attack.

2. Start of tori's arm action.

3. Continuation of arm action.

4. Striking action.

Grab around the neck

Uke grabs tori around the neck from behind. This is a common attack used by uke when an opppent has her back to him. Depending on uke's aims, the move can control tori, render her unconscious or kill her.

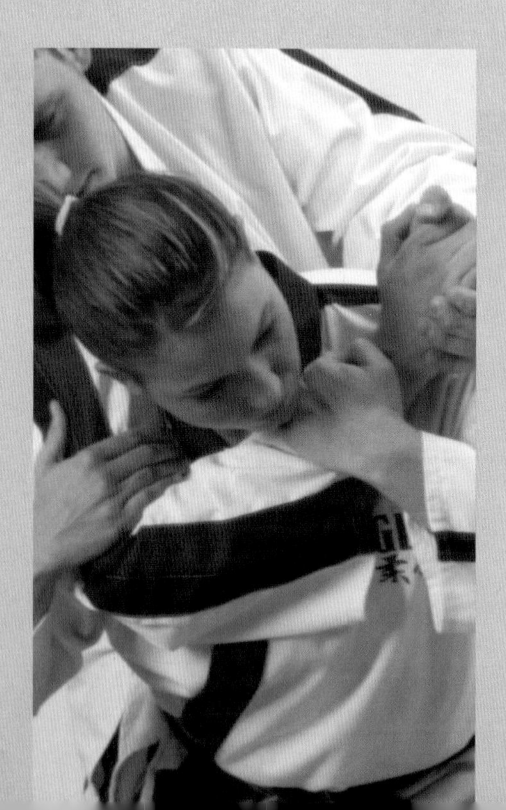

Seoi otoshi (shoulder drop throw)

Tori grabs uke's arm which is around the neck and drops down on one knee, twisting her body in order to flip uke off her back.

1. Attacking position.

2. Tori's hand position.

3. Body positioning.

4. Completion of throw

Sukui nage (scoop throw)

Tori leans forward while simultaneously stepping sideways. Placing the left leg behind uke, tori reaches down and takes both of uke's legs, lifting straight back and falling on uke.

1. Attacking position.

2. Tori's hand position.

3. Body positioning.

4. Leg grab.

5. Throwing action.

1. Attacking position.

Ude gatame (armlock)

Uke bends forwards and steps sideways rotating the shoulders. Taking uke's wrist, tori pulls the head free. Keeping one hand on the wrist, tori places the other hand on the back of uke's elbow, pushing uke straight down to the ground with a slight semi-circular action. Tori kneels on uke's elbow, this arm disables uke by pulling back on the wrist.

2. Tori's hand position.

3. Body positioning.

4. Continuation of body positioning.

5. Hand placement.

6. Direction of push.

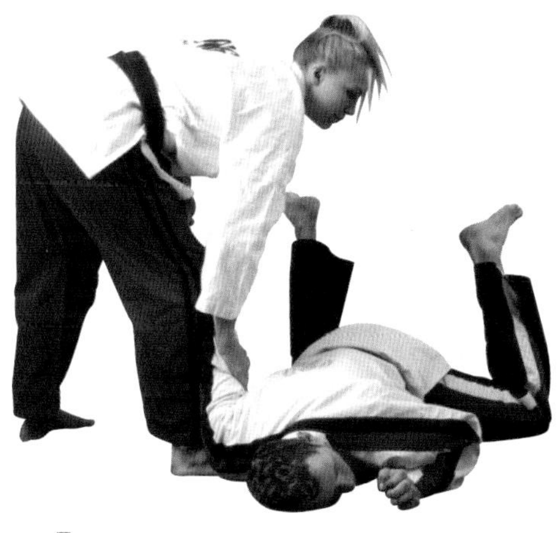

7. Completion of technique.

1. Attacking position.

Yama arashi (mountain storm throw)

Tori grabs uke's arm. Pulling it forwards to minimise the pressure on the neck, tori steps slightly sideways towards uke's free arm and stands on one leg, pulls forwards and sweeps back with the other leg.

2. Tori's hand position.

3. Start of throwing action.

4. Completion of throwing action.

Defence against kicks

Predominantly there are three methods of kicking. There is a front kick, which normally uses the top of the foot or the toes and involves taking the leg straight up into uke's body. There is the roundhouse kick, which involves swinging the leg and foot in a semi-circular motion. Lastly there is the straight kick, which is delivered by the side of the foot, normally to the lower half of uke's body. Most kicks that are effective do not travel above waist height. It is possible to deliver kicks to the chest, neck and face, but inevitably power is lost and tori's balance is compromised.

Defence against a roundhouse kick

Tori blocks uke's leg with a downward block of the forearm. Once the kick is stopped by the block, tori turns inwards towards uke's kicking leg and, with the spare hand, either grasps the jacket or pushes uke's face, then hooks in between uke's legs and behind the supporting leg. As tori does this, she pushes uke's head so that he falls backwards to the ground, or alternatively holds on to uke's clothing and drives down, landing on top of uke.

Kosoto gake (minor outer hook)

Tori blocks the swinging leg, changing it to a grip, then hooks the outside of uke's standing leg with her own leg driving backwards at the same time, pushing with the heel of the hand into uke's face.

1. Starting position.

2. Uke's kick and tori's block.

3. Tori's hand position.

4. Pushing action.

5. Completion of technique.

Hiza atemi waza (knee strike)

Tori blocks uke's leg with one arm and immediately drives her knee up into uke's groin.

1. Starting position.

2. Uke's kick and tori's block.

3. Striking action.

Sasae tsurikomi ashi

Tori blocks the swinging leg and changes the blocking hand to grip uke's leg. The spare hand grabs uke's head at the back of the neck. Tori blocks uke's standing leg with the sole of the foot and pulls uke over the blocking leg.

1. Starting position.

2. Uke's kick and tori's block.

3. Tori's hand and body position.

4. Completion of technique.

Defence against a front kick

Cross block

Tori makes a fist with both hands to tighten the forearm muscles. Tori then crosses her wrists and endeavours to block the shin of uke's kicking leg.

Sweep support leg with de ashi barai or kosoto gari

Tori blocks using a cross block then hooks with the instep of her right leg behind (for kosoto gari) or to the side (for de ashi barai) of uke's support leg, while simultaneously pushing backwards.

1. Starting position.

2. Uke's kick and tori's block.

3. Completion of technique.

Ankle twist

After the initial movement is blocked, tori grasps uke's ankle and the toes of the striking leg and twists.

1. Starting position.

2. Uke's kick and tori's block.

3. Gripping action.

4. Twisting action.

5. Completion of technique.

Front kick to the groin

Using a cross block to stop the kick, tori steps for avoidance then returns with a kick of her own to the groin.

1. Starting position.

2. Uke's kick and tori's block.

3. Avoidance step.

4. Kicking action.

5. Completion of technique.

Ashi dori (leg grab)

This is a foot sweep, used as a counter against a kick. Tori blocks with a cross-arm action and then holds the blocked leg with one hand. At the same time, she steps towards uke, grabbing his lapel with her other hand. With a lifting action that takes the weight off uke's standing leg, tori sweeps the standing leg sideways.

1. Starting position.

2. Uke's kick and tori's block.

3. Gripping action.

4. Stepping action.

5. Lifting action.

6. Sweeping action.

chapter 6:

Newaza (ground techniques)

In a fight, it is quite usual to end up on the ground. In a one-on-one situation there are many techniques that can be used. The positions normally are either tori on her back with uke on top, or uke on his back with tori on top. With ju jitsu technique there is a wide range of moves that can be used when tori is supine (on the back).

The ground-fighting techniques shown here involve strangles, neck locks and leg locks. The objective and skills of ground-work fighting involve being able to control an opponent before he or she attempts any of these techniques. Control is normally gained by using the legs and body weight, together with the positioning of the hands. Strangles are used because the neck area is very vulnerable in ground-fighting situations. The main principle used is the exertion of pressure on the carotid artery, situated either side of the neck. The artery is protected by the neck muscles, but the action of a grip tends to move the muscles to one side.

Tori in a supine position (hold-downs)

All the techniques shown are attempted when tori positions herself immediately into a defensive grappling position on her back and gets uke between the legs.

These strangles can also be executed when tori is on top of uke, sitting astride his stomach. Quite often the strangle will be initiated while tori is underneath and she will use her legs to turn uke over.

Shimi waza (strangles)

The objective of these strangle techniques is to exert pressure on the carotid arteries, which are located in the neck below the earlobe, following the line of the jaw. It is assumed that the opponent or aggressor will be wearing normal clothing – a shirt with collars or a coat, represented by a gi.

Gyaku juji jime (reverse cross strangle)

Uke is between tori's legs and is being controlled by tori with a do jime technique. Do jime is a squeezing scissor action of the legs. Tori reaches across with her right hand to uke's collar, with her fingers inside the collar and does the same to the other lapel with the other hand. The grip needs to be deep enough so as to place the cutting edge of the inside of the arm level with the carotid artery. Tori then pulls uke's head towards her. This creates a scissor action against the carotid arteries and, if positioned correctly, uke will for training purposes submit, or in a real-life threatening situation become unconscious.

Ryote jime (double-handed strangle)

Tori grasps the outside of uke's collar on either side of the neck, positioning the knuckles level with the carotid arteries. Tori then rotates her fists inwards towards the carotid arteries. She then lifts her legs to uke's shoulders, crossing her legs and applying pressure with her fists.

Tsuri komi jime (thrusting strangle)

Tori grasps the far lapel of uke's jacket with the thumb inside and grips the opposite lapel with fingers inside and the hand turned so that the thumb is pointing down. Tori then pushes the lapel under uke's chin and drives into the throat area. The knuckle grip is level with the carotid artery to apply the strangle.

Sode guruma jime (sleeve wheel strangle)

Tori throws her forearm across the back of uke's neck and the other forearm goes under uke's throat. Tori's hands then grasp her own sleeves; quite often this is a choke on the windpipe rather than being applied to the carotid arteries.

1. Standing technique.

Katsugi jime (shoulder carry strangle)

Tori places her fingers inside uke's collar. With the other hand she places the thumb inside. Tori then releases uke's body with her legs and, as uke tries to stand up or escape sideways, tori spins her body and applies the strangle against the carotid artery with the outside of her arm and the thumb of the other hand. This can be performed standing or on the ground.

2. Ground-fighting technique.

Sangaku jime (triangle strangle)

Tori's legs release the waist grip on uke, tori then hooks the back of her knee on the back of one of uke's shoulders. Tori then transfers the back of the knee on the other foot. While maintaining uke's arm tori then exerts pressure on uke's neck by pushing down on the hooking leg.

Gyaku hishigi (dislocation by elongation)

Tori takes her arm over the back of uke's neck, gripping the head while maintaining control with the legs around uke's waist. Submission or damage is achieved by pushing down with the legs and pulling uke's head in the opposite direction. The grip on the head requires tori to grasp her own hands at the same time in order to gain more control.

Gyaku ude gurame (reverse arm entanglement)

Tori maintains the grip with her legs around uke's waist and grasps one of uke's wrists. Tori then takes her arm over uke's triceps area. Twisting and then taking hold of her own wrist, she then applies pressure by pushing back on the wrist. This action tends to be a shoulder lock.

Ashi kannuki (leg bolt lock)

Tori releases do jime (scissor action) from around the waist and applies do jime to one of uke's legs. Tori places the back of her knee on to the shin of the opposite leg and the foot of the same leg hooks the top of uke's foot. Pressure is put on the knee by pushing the legs straight down and simultaneously pulling the hook foot sideways.

Uke in a defensive posture

Uke is lying flat, face down in a defensive posture. This position is normally adopted by uke having been thrown to the ground. The position is purely defensive. Tori can make a number of moves to control uke.

Hadaku jime (naked strangle)

Tori jumps on uke's back and maintains control by hooking her legs under the thigh. Tori then places her chest on uke's back and pushes her body into the ground, simultaneously lifting her hooked-in legs on to uke's thighs. This action exerts pressure on the spinal area. Simultaneously, tori slides a straight hand under uke's chin and grabs her other hand. Tori applies pressure to the back of the neck by pulling back using her own chest as a block.

Kata ha jime (single collar strangle)

Tori jumps on uke's back, hooks her legs in and pushes her hips into the small of uke's back. Tori slides her hand under uke's chin and grasps the thumb inside, fingers outside, endeavouring to get her wrist action level with the furthest carotid artery region of the neck. Tori's other hand comes under uke's armpit and, with the palm down on the back of uke's neck, tori then pushes the head forward and rotates in a semi-circular action, which applies the strangle.

chapter 7:

Defence against weapons

Certain situations, especially when a weapon is involved, require immediate action. It is important to assess the situation as quickly as possible and try to escape with little or no personal injury. This may require varied levels of pain or injury to the aggressor.

If a weapon is involved, this generally suggests that the situation is serious. Distraction can be a very useful tactic against an armed assailant. By distracting or disorientating an attacker, you can gain valuable time by taking his or her mind off the intended action.

Subtle movement, such as a slight hand movement prior to a kick, can be just enough to give the victim an advantage. When dealing with an armed aggressor, care should be taken not to provoke or startle them into action.

A weapon could be a knife or an instrument such as a club, stick or baseball bat. Knife attacks are normally thrusts to the body in a straight line, in a half circle or in a downward blow action.

Defence against knife attacks

A knife attack is most likely to be a downward strike or straight thrust.

Naname zuki (oblique slash)

Uke uses a downward movement when attacking with a knife.

Ippon seoi nage (one-arm shoulder throw)

Tori blocks the right-handed attack from uke with her left forearm and turns the hand to grip the wrist or sleeve. Tori steps forward with her right foot and swings the left foot behind, placing her feet approximately shoulder-width apart. At the same time, tori's right arm is placed under uke's right armpit, positioning tori's inner elbow joint into uke's armpit region, this arm is used as a prop. Tori bends her knees, keeping her back straight. Tori pulls uke on to his back, using the sleeve grip, then straightens her legs and rotates her upper body, pulling in a big circular movement to offload uke on to the ground.

1. Tori's blocking action.

2. Gripping action.

3. Lifting action.

4. Throwing action.

Kote waza (wrist lock)

As uke attempts to bring the knife down and stab tori in the left side of tori's neck, tori steps backwards with her right leg to avoid contact with the knife. With her left hand, tori pushes uke's hand in the direction it is already travelling i.e. downwards, and grips uke's wrist. Tori then uses her right hand to enhance the grip while stepping back with the left foot. Tori turns uke's wrist in an anti-clockwise direction, causing uke to fall to the ground. This can also be used against a thrusting action.

1. Tori's avoidance and blocking action.

Tori maintains the grip with her left hand, when uke is on the ground, slides her right hand under uke's arm and secures a grip on uke's wrist. Tori then uses both hands to pull and the shoulder to push until uke's wrist is bent on the floor. This causes uke to release the knife (if he hasn't already). Tori uses her left hand to remove the knife. Tori must not release uke until the knife has been removed.

2. Gripping action.

3. Completion of tcchniquo.

Defence against stick attacks

Blunt instruments such as a club are often used as weapons. The most frequent attack is the baseball swing, and to deal with this Tai otoshi or Makikomi can be used.

Tai otoshi (body drop)

As uke swings the bat towards tori's head or body, tori steps forwards, getting as close to uke's body as possible. Tori does not attempt to block the bat as personal injury is inevitable, instead tori blocks uke's arms and hands which are holding the bat. Tori simultaneously swings her left leg behind her and, grabbing uke's wrist, rotates in the direction of the swing. A wide leg stance is adopted.

1. Tori's blocking action.

2. Body and hand positions.

3. Completion of throw.

Conclusion

It would be impossible to include all the variations and techniques of ju jitsu in this handbook as there is insufficient space, but the waza shown are some of the most effective. However, to achieve knowledge of the technique and use them as a fighting skill requires training of a high standard. I would recommend that if you wish to attain the skills of ju jitsu you join a ju jitsu club. Throughout the world there are many different styles of ju jitsu, some concentrate more on throwing, some more on blows and locks. All require a considerable degree of study. Finally, I would also like to remind you that in untrained hands and without proper control ju jitsu can be very dangerous.

Target Areas

The areas that run down the centre of the body tend to be the most vulnerable targets. By inflicting pain, you can slow down, control or cause damage to an assailant. The focus of the assailant becomes directed to the area of pain and this makes them more vulnerable. In training, accuracy is the important factor. The body's warning system, pain, causes the body to react; no reaction suggests the level of force needs to be increased. It is important to realise that certain techniques, in certain circumstances, are lethal!

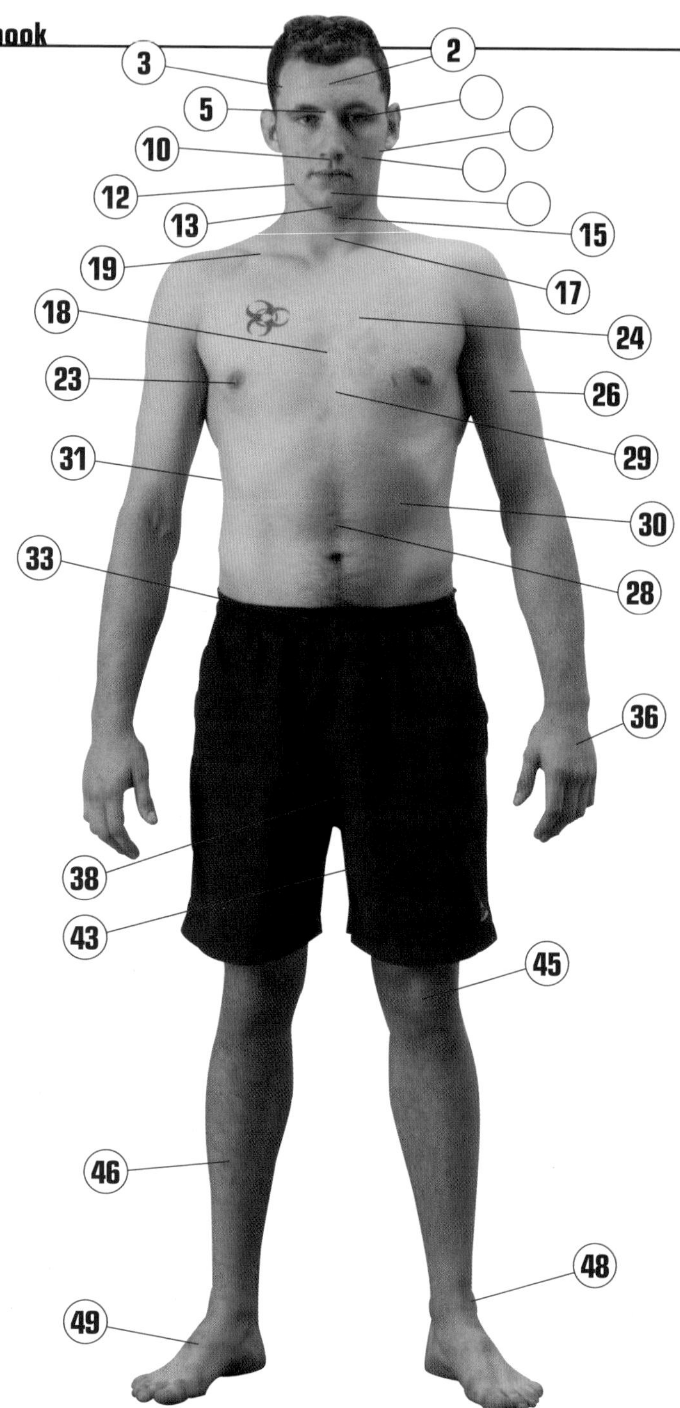

1) The top of the head

The area where the frontal cranial bones join the skull is weak. A hard blow to this area causes damage to the cranial cavity, which could result in a haemorrhage, unconsciousness and, in severe cases, death.

2) The forehead

Dependent on its force, a blow may result in whiplash, cerebral haemorrhaging or death.

3) The temples

The skull is weak at the temples; an artery and large nerve are situated in this region. A blow to this region could result in unconsciousness and concussion. If, however, the artery is severed a huge haemorrhage could result in a coma or death.

4) The eyes

A poke in the eye by a finger, thumb or knuckle causes watering and blurred vision and can be very useful to disorientate and slow down an attacker. A forceful poke can result in temporary blindness. Death could result if the eyes are penetrated into the brain.

5) Between the eyes

If it is hard enough, a strike at the top of the nose could knock out an attacker.

6) The cheekbones

A hard blow to the cheekbone could cause a fracture.

7) The ears

A very hard slap to both the ears with cupped hands can cause the eardrums to burst and cause concussion.

8) Below the earlobes

Due to the nerves situated in this area, pressure from a finger, thumb or knuckle in a screwing action can cause intense pain.

9) The nose

A blow to the nose causes intense pain and may cause the eyes to water and therefore has a disorientation factor. The thin bones in the nose break quite easily.

10) The septum

This is the cartilage situated between the nostrils. Pressing hard in this area can cause an assailant to fall over.

11) The hollow between the chin and bottom lip

A thumb or knuckle to this area causes pain.

12) The jaw

A blow to the jaw, dependent on the force exerted, could cause it to break or dislocate. If the nerve is pinched, one side of the face becomes paralysed.

13) The chin

A blow to the chin can have serious effects; it can cause paralysis, concussion and unconsciousness. The force transmitted through the jawbone can radiate to the back of the brain and affect the cardiac and respiratory mechanisms that are controlled in that region of the brain.

14) The base of the skull

Due to the jarring effect caused by a blow in this region, unconsciousness, concussion or a brain haemorrhage possibly leading to death could occur.

15) The throat

A sharp blow to the throat is very painful and disorienting, it also can be lethal! The amount of damage caused depends on the impetus of the blow. This depends on the extent of the threat to the victim's own life.

16) The neck

The obvious strangles are either cutting off the air supply by targeting the windpipe, or cutting off the blood supply to the brain by targeting the carotid arteries. A blow to either side of the neck using a ridge hand can be very effective. It can cause involuntary muscle spasms, intense pain and unconsciousness. A strong blow to the back of the neck can cause whiplash, concussion or possibly a broken neck and death.

17) The sternal notch

This is the hollow below the chin, at the base of the throat. A finger or thumb pressed in this area causes pain (there are no muscles in this area so it is relatively weak).

18) The sternum

The breastbone is situated in the centre of the chest. A blow to this region can cause serious damage and may wind an aggressor.

19) The collarbones

A hard strike to the collarbone will cause it to break and prevent the use of the arm on the affected side.

20) The shoulders

A strike to the tip of the shoulder, especially the tip of the bone, will cause severe pain. A bundle of nerves is located in front of each shoulder joint, a blow to this region causes severe pain and can numb the arm.

21) The armpits

The arms usually protect this area. However a large nerve lies in the armpit close to the skin, and a blow or jab with a knuckle into the armpit can cause extreme pain and partial paralysis.

22) The sides of the torso

The region on the side of the body, underneath the armpit, is very painful when hit.

23) The nipples

This is a sensitive area: a pinch, twist and pull action is very effective. A strike to this area is also painful due to the large number of nerves in the region.

24) The chest

A jolt to the heart can stun an aggressor. This should only be used in extreme circumstances because of the potential damage it can cause.

25) The spine

If the spinal cord is severed, the result is paralysis or death.

26) The biceps

This is a particularly good target if an assailant has a weapon. A strike to the biceps is painful and can paralyse the arm.

27) The triceps

This is the area at the back of the upper arm. A pinch to this area can be very effective.

28) The solar plexus

A network of nerves is located within the stomach area. If this area is targeted it will cause immense pain and can have a paralysing effect. A deep strike using the elbow can slow down or stop an assailant.

29) The diaphragm

A blow to this region can adversely affect an assailant's breathing and could result in unconsciousness due to respiratory failure.

30) The floating rib region

Just below the ribcage, where the floating ribs are located, is a painful area for most kinds of kick or strike. Internal damage can be caused, the lungs could be punctured or damage could be caused to the liver.

31) The side of the ribcage

A strike to this area will cause pain and is relatively easy to target. The strike can be carried out with the heel of the palm.

32) The back

Aiming for the kidney region, either side of the spine in the small of the back, use a palm-heel strike or kick to cause severe pain. A blow to this region induces shock and could cause internal damage to the kidneys.

33) The abdomen

A strike just below the navel causes shock, unconsciousness, and internal bleeding.

34) The elbows

Often an attacker will reach out to grab or strike causing their arm to be straight. If tori holds the wrist and strikes the elbow joint with the palm of the hand, it is very painful and the elbow may break. On the ground the opportunity may arise to kick or stamp on the elbow. There are various locks that can be applied to the elbow joint.

35) The forearms

A strike just below the elbow, where the radial nerve is located, can disable the arm.

36) The back of the hand

Nerves pass over the bones in the hand making them very sensitive. A strike on the hand is very painful and can easily break the bones, making the hand ineffective.

37) The hipbones

A blow to the front of the hipbones will cause pain. Alternatively, digging the thumbs in deep just above the hipbones is also very painful.

38) The groin

This area is very sensitive, particularly for men, and because of this men consciously protect the testicles. A strike to the groin can disable an assailant. Strike up between the legs with either the knee or foot. Even a relatively light tap with the hand can cause serious pain. On the ground, the opportunity may arise to stamp in this area. A strong blow can cause unconsciousness and shock.

39) The base of the buttocks

There are many nerves in this region, so a sharp blow with the knee could certainly slow down an attacker.

40) The wrists

The inner parts of the wrists are painful if struck hard using the knuckles. These areas can also be targeted for locks.

41) The fingers

Stamp on the fingers or pull them apart. The bones in the fingers will break if struck hard.

42) The outer thighs

Just above the knee a large nerve passes near the surface; a strike to this area using a knee strike or heel kick can incapacitate the leg and cause an assailant to drop to the ground.

43) The inner thighs

Inside the legs just below the groin makes a good target, especially for a hard pinch.

44) The hamstrings

A hard strike can cause muscle spasms and paralyse the area.

45) The knees

The knee joint is a very weak joint; it is also easily accessible. If accurately targeted it can be totally disabling. The knee is one of the primary target areas because when an aggressor attacks he or she usually steps forward, leaving the knee open for attack. If the back of the knee is targeted the assailant is likely to fall to the ground as the knee gives way. Locks can also be applied to the knee joint.

46) The shin bones

A hard kick on the shin is painful, even more so if it is followed by a scrape down the shin and a stamp on the foot. If kicked hard enough, the shin will break.

47) The calves

This target is below the back of the knees, just above the central part of the lower leg. If kicked hard, particularly with the heel, it is very painful and mobility is inhibited.

48) The ankles

A hard kick to the bony protuberance on the inside or outside of the ankle is very painful. Also stamping down hard in that region at the back of the ankle can cause damage to the Achilles tendon which, if torn, incapacitates the assailant.

49) The feet

Using the full body weight on the foot or the heel, a stamp can be directed on to the upper arch of the foot or the big toe, and can be very painful.

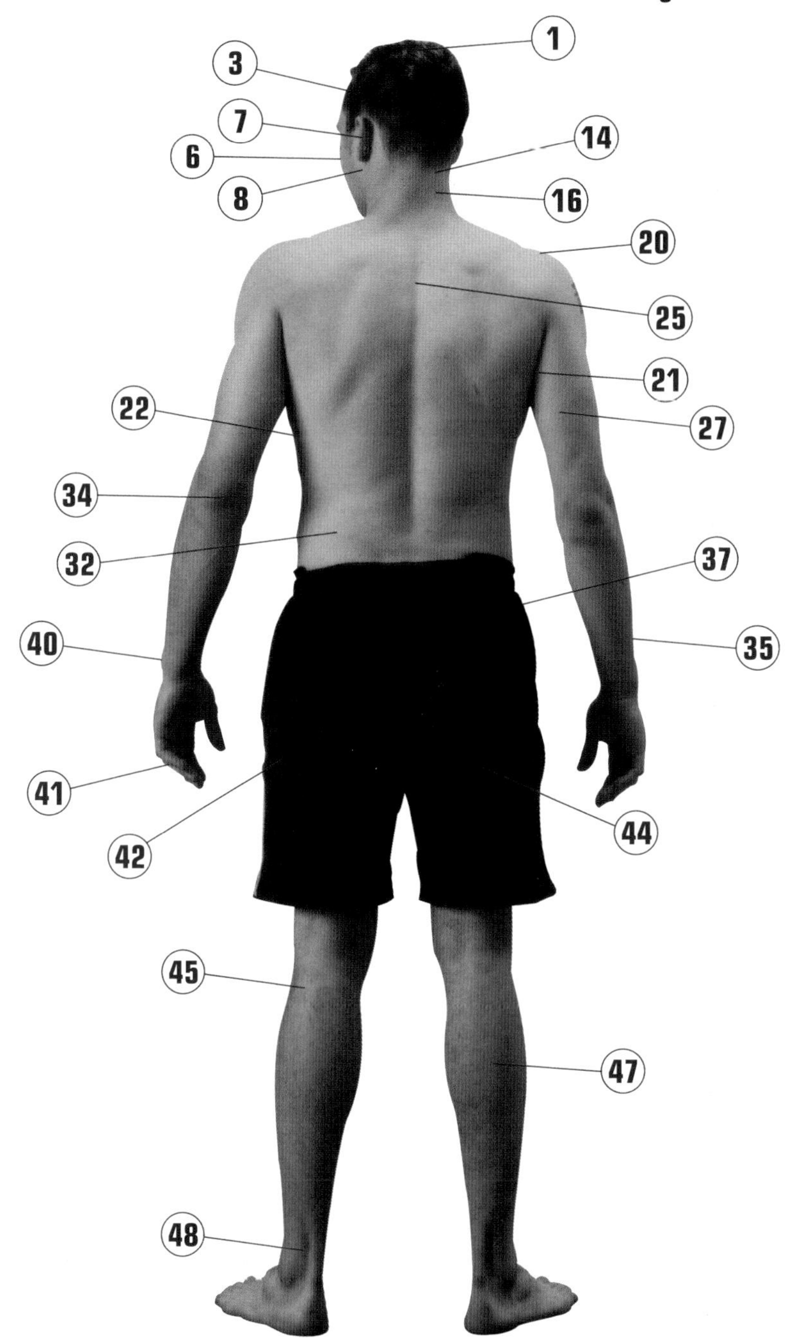
1
3
7
6
8
14
16
20
25
21
22
27
34
32
37
40
35
41
42
44
45
47
48

Glossary

A

Age uke - raising block
Ago tsuki - upper cut
Aikido - means 'the way of spirit and mind'. Dr Morihei Ueshiba extracted what he felt were the best techniques of daitoryu aiki ju jitsu and combined them with what he deemed to be the better techniques of the various forms of ju jitsu he had learned, to create present-day aikido.
Ashi - foot or leg
Ashi dori - leg grab
Ashi gatame - leg armlock
Ashi guruma - leg wheel
Ashi kannuki - leg bolt lock
Ashi kansetsu waza - leg locks
Ashi waza - foot or leg technique
Atama - head
Atama hishigi - head crush
Atama waza - head strike
Atemi waza - striking techniques These include kicks and strikes using the hands, feet, elbows, knees, particularly targeting weak areas of the body; often known as the vital points.

B

Budo - martial arts

C

Chikura kurabe - an ancient wrestling sport
Choku zuki - standard fist punch

D

Daitoryu aiki ju jitsu - taken from ju jitsu, General Shinra Saburo Yoshimutsu devised a pure form of educational exercises as a way of advancing his military officers mentally, physically and spiritually. Daitoryu aiki ju jitsu was kept a secret and only passed down to a hereditary successor.
Dan - black belt rank. A system used to exhibit the proficiency of the wearer of the black belt.
Deashi barai/harai - advancing foot sweep
Do - the way or path

Do jime - body scissors or trunk strangle. The torso of an opponent is held between the legs, feet are usually crossed.
Dojo - the place were ju jitsu is practised.

E

Empi - elbow
Empi uchi - elbow strike
Eri - collar or lapel
Eri gatame - collar hold

F

Fumi komi - stamp kick

G

Gake - hook
Gan men tsuki - punch to the face
Garami - entangle
Gatame - hold or tighten
Gedan barai - downward block
Gi - the specially designed clothes worn when participating in martial arts.
Go no sen - beating an opponent by reacting to their attack and countering them (responding to the attack rather than pre-empting it).
Go-shin-jutsu-karate - self-defence art of the open hand
Gyaku - reverse
Gyaku atama waza - reverse head strike
Gyaku empi uchi - reverse elbow strike
Gyaku hishigi - dislocation by elongation
Gyaku juji jime - reverse cross strangle
Gyaku morote gari - reverse double leg grab
Gyaku ogoshi - reverse major hip throw
Gyaku uki otoshi - reverse floating drop

H

Hadaka - naked
Hadaka jime - naked strangle
Haishu uchi - back-hand strike
Hajime! - 'begin', a refereeing command used to start or re-start a contest

Hane - spring
Hane goshi - spring hip
Hane makikomi- winding spring hip
Hansoku make - disqualification. A contest is lost by committing a major infraction or accumulating minor infractions.
Hantei! - the refereeing call for a judge's decision. The winner is determined by a majority of the three referees' decisions. On the call of 'Hantei!' a flag is raised in a corresponding colour to one of the competitors.
Hara gatame - stomach armlock
Harai/barai - sweep
Harai goshi - sweeping hip
Harai makikomi - winding sweeping hip
Harai tsurikomi ashi - sweeping lift-pull ankle
Hiza - knee
Hiza atemi - knee strike
Hiza gatame - knee armlock
Hiza guruma - knee wheel
Hiza hishigi - knee crush or dislocation
Hiza uchi - knee strike
Hon kesa gatame - basic scarf hold

I

Ippon - although in literal terms ippon means one complete point it is given the score value of 10.
Ippon seoi nage - one-arm shoulder throw

J

Jigoro Kano - the founder of modern judo.
Jigotai - defensive posture
Jigouku jime - hell strangle
Jime - strangle or choke
Jitsu - art
Joshibu - women's section
Ju - gentle or non-resistant
Judo - literally means 'way of non-resistance' referred to as the 'gentle way'. A martial art and sport developed through the adaptation of several styles of ju jitsu and enhanced with Jigoro Kano's own philosophies.
Juji gatame - cross armlock
Jujitsuka - someone who practises ju jitsu.
Jujitsu/Jujutsu - combat using the empty hand, without weapons

K

Kaeshi waza - counter techniques. A reaction to an opponent's attack.
Kaesu - to block an opponent's attack and execute a counter attack
Kami shiho gatame - upper four quarters
Kan - building or hall
Kani basami - leg scissors
Kani garami - crab entanglement
Kansetsu waza - joint techniques. In judo competition the only joint that may be locked is the elbow joint.
Kata - specific sequences of techniques. It also means 'shoulder' e.g. kata gatame, or 'single' e.g. kata juji jime.
Kata ashi hishigi - single leg crush or dislocation
Kata gatame - shoulder hold
Kata guruma - shoulder wheel
Kata ha jime - single collar strangle
Kata juji jime - single cross strangle
Katsugi gatame - shoulder carry armlock
Keri waza - kicking techniques
Kesa garami - scarf armlock
Kesa gatame - scarf hold. Also known as hon kesa gatame.
Kesa gatame kubi hishigi - scarf hold neck dislocation
Ki - is the inner spirit, a person's drive or energy. It enables a jujitsuka to take control of a situation in a relaxed manner.
Kibishi gaeshi - heel trip
Ko - minor. Teaching, study and learning.
Koka - a score that is almost a yuko, it has the value of three points.
Koshi - hip
Koshi guruma - hip wheel
Koshi jime - hip strangle
Koshi waza - hip techniques
Kosoto gake - minor outer hook
Kosoto gari - minor outer reap
Kote - wrist
Kote dori - wrist trap/grab
Kote gaeshi - wrist reverse
Kouchi gake - minor inner hook
Kouchi gari - minor inner reap
Kubi hishigi - dislocation neck lock or neck crush
Kubi kansetsu waza - spine locks
Kuzure - means broken but actually refers to a modified technique
Kuzure kami shiho gatami - broken upper four quarters

Kuzure kesa gatame - broken scarf hold
Kuzure kesa kubi hishigi - broken scarf hold neck crush
Kuzushi - the action of breaking an opponent's balance in preparation for a throw
Kyu - student grade

M

Mae - front
Mae geri - front kick
Maitta! - 'I give up', verbal submission
Mawashi geri - roundhouse kick
Makikomi waza - wrapping techniques
Makura kesa gatame - pillow scarf hold
Matte! - 'break' or 'wait', a command used to stop a contest temporarily
Morote gari - double-leg grab
Morote shuto uchi - double-handed knife-edge strike
Morote seoi nage - two-handed shoulder throw
Mune - chest
Mune gatame - chest hold

N

Nagekomi - repetitive throwing practice
Nagashi uke - sweeping block
Nage waza - throwing techniques
Nami juji jime - standard cross strangle
Naname zuki - oblique slash
Newaza - ground techniques. Techniques executed in various ground grappling positions.
Nidan kosoto gake - two-step minor outer hook
Nidan kosoto gari - two-step minor outer reaping

O

Obi - belt
Ogoshi - major hip throw
Oguruma - major wheel
Okuriashi harai/barai - double-foot sweep
Okuri eri jime - sliding-collar strangle
Osae Hishigi - dislocation in immobilisation, necklock
Osaekomi - a referee's call, which signifies that hold down is on and timing should begin

Osaekomi waza - holding techniques
Osoto gake - major outer hook
Osoto gari - major outer reap
Osoto guruma - major wheel
Osoto makikomi - major outer winding
Osoto otoshi - major outer drop
Otoshi - to drop
Ouchi gake - major inner hook
Ouchi gari - major inner reaping

R

Randori - free practice. A training method which allows both participants the opportunity to try and develop techniques in standing and ground work
Rei - bow, a mark of respect
Renraku waza - combination techniques. Several techniques in quick succession without a break.
Renzoku waza - continuous use of combination technique, one leading into the other.
Ritsurei - standing bow
Ryo ashi hishigi - double-leg crush or dislocation
Ryote jime - double-hand strangle

S

Sangaku gatame - triangle hold
Sangaku jime - triangle strangle
Sasae - to support/prop
Sasae tsurikomi ashi - propping drawing ankle
Sensei - ju jitsu instructor or coach
Septum - the cartilage situated between the nostrils
Seoi otoshi - shoulder drop
Shiai - a contest
Shido - a penalty
Shime waza - strangulation techniques
Shuto uchi - knife-hand strike
Sode - sleeve
Sode guruma jime - sleeve wheel strangle
Sono mama! - 'hold your position' or 'freeze'. This is called by the referee, while simultaneously touching both competitors to temporarily stop the contest with the competitors remaining in the same position. This is usually done to check for injury or to award a penalty
Sore made! - 'finished'. This signifies the end of the contest.
Soto ude uke - outside forearm block

Sternal notch - the hollow at the base of the throat
Sternum - breastbone
Sukui nage - scoop throw
Sumi gaeshi - corner throw
Sumi otoshi - corner drop
Sumai - an ancient form of sumo
Sumo - Japanese wrestling
Shuto te - knife hand
Sutemi waza - sacrifice techniques

T

Tachi waza - techniques executed in a standing position
Tai otoshi - body drop
Tani otoshi - valley drop
Tai otoshi uchi makikomi - body drop inner winding throw
Tatame - exercise mat
Tate hishigi - standing dislocation
Tate shiho gatame - lengthwise four-quarters holding
Tawara gaeshi - rice-bail throw
Te - hand or arm
Te guruma - hand wheel
Teisho uchi - palm-heel strike
Te otoshi - hand drop
Tettsui uchi - hammer-fist strike
Te waza - hand techniques
Tobi geri - flying kick
Toketa! - 'hold broken'. A call made by the referee while waving his/her hand from side to side to indicate that the hold is no longer effective and to let the timekeeper know to stop the oaeskomi clock
Tomoe nage - circular throw, often refered to as stomach throw
Tori - the person executing the technique
Triangular grip block - a method used to break a double-lapel grip
Tsubame gaeshi - swallow-swoop counter
Tsuri goshi - lifting hip throw, also known as fishing hip throw
Tsurikomi goshi - lift-pull hip throw
Tsurikomi jimi - thrusting strangle

U

Uchikomi - Repetitive technique. A form of training designed to develop skills by repetition.
Uchimata - inner-thigh throw
Uchimata makikomi - winding inner thigh
Ude - arm
Ude barai - forearm sweeping block

Ude gaeshi - arm roll
Ude garami - entangled armlock
Ude gatame- armlock
Uke - is the person being thrown
Uke waza - blocking techniques
Ukemi - breakfall techniques
Uki goshi - floating hip
Uki otoshi - floating drop
Uki waza - floating throw
Uraken uchi - back fist strike
Ura kote - reverse wrist lock
Ura nage - rear throw
Ushiro - backwards, rear
Ushiro goshi - rear hip
Ushiro geri - rear kick
Ushiro kesa gatame - reverse scarf hold
Utsuri goshi - changing hip

W

Waza - technique (i.e. nage waza, throwing technique; tachi waza standing technique; newaza, ground technique; atemi waza, striking techniques)
Waza ari - a near ippon score. It has the value of seven points.
Waza ari awasete ippon - actually means 'combined one point'. If a competitor achieves two waza ari scores, by whatever means, it is deemed to be of the same value as an outright ippon.
Waki gatame - armpit armlock

Y

Yama arashi - mountain storm, the name of a specific throw
Yoko - side
Yoko gake - side hook
Yoko geri - side kick
Yoko guruma - side wheel
Yoko otoshi - side drop
Yoko shiho gatame - side four quarters
Yoko sutemi waza - side sacrifice technique
Yoko wakare - side separation
Yoshi! - 'continue'. The referee's call to resume the contest following a sono mama situation.
Yuko - a score that is almost a waza ari. A 5-point score.

Z

Zarei - kneeling bow
Zori - footwear similar to flip-flops, traditionally made of straw

index

bibliography and credits

Sources

Aida, H.: **Kodokan Judo,** pub. W. Foulsham & Co Ltd

Kashiwazaki, K. & Nakanishi, H.: **Attacking Judo**, pub. Ippon Books

Kawaishi, M.: **My Method of Judo,** pub. W. Foulsham & Co Ltd

Kawamura, T. & Daigo, T.: **Kodokan Dictionary,** pub.The Foundation of the Kodokan

Leggett, T.P.: **The Demonstration of Gentleness,** pub.W. Foulsham & Co Ltd

Mack, C.J.: **Karate Test Technique,** pub.Pelham Books

Varmuttu, R.A.: **Unarmed Combat,** pub.W. Foulsham & Co Ltd

Yamada, S.: **Aikido,** pub.Senta Yamada Ltd

About the author

Roy Inman OBE, 8th Dan

For 40 years Roy Inman has been involved in various forms of martial arts and is currently a Senior Instructor at the Budokwai Martial Arts Club in London and High Performance Coach at the University of Bath. He has coached many judo players to Olympic and World Championship medals.

Acknowledgements

I would like to extend my sincere thanks to Michelle Holt, a member of the British Judo and Ju jitsu Squads, two times World Sports Ju jitsu Champion and two times WCJJO World Ju jitsu Champion, without whose help this book would not exist. I would also like to thank Andy Burns and Sian Wilson, members of the British Judo Squad for their expertise in compiling technical photographs. Thank you also to Carol, my wife, for her continued support.